Accounting in the LEAN Enterprise

Providing *Simple*, Practical, and Decision-Relevant Information

Accounting in the LEAN Enterprise

Providing *Simple*, Practical, and Decision-Relevant Information

GLORIA MᶜVAY

FRANCES KENNEDY

ROSEMARY FULLERTON

CRC Press
Taylor & Francis Group
Boca Raton London New York

CRC Press is an imprint of the
Taylor & Francis Group, an **informa** business

A PRODUCTIVITY PRESS BOOK

CRC Press
Taylor & Francis Group
6000 Broken Sound Parkway NW, Suite 300
Boca Raton, FL 33487-2742

Printed on acid-free paper
Version Date: 20130412

International Standard Book Number-13: 978-1-4200-8858-8 (Paperback)

Library of Congress Cataloging-in-Publication Data

McVay, Gloria.
    Accounting in the lean enterprise : providing simple, practical, and decision-relevant Information / Gloria McVay, Frances Kennedy, Rosemary Fullerton.
    pages cm
    Includes bibliographical references and index.
    ISBN 978-1-4200-8858-8 (pbk. : alk. paper)
    1. Lean manufacturing--Accounting. 2. Managerial accounting. 3. Cost control. 4. Production control. I. Kennedy, Frances A. II. Fullerton, Rosemary. III. Title.

HF5686.M3M39 2013
658.4'012--dc23   2013008021

Visit the Taylor & Francis Web site at
http://www.taylorandfrancis.com

and the CRC Press Web site at
http://www.crcpress.com

Contents

SECTION III CONTROLS AND TRANSITION

Foreword

Lean accounting has gained greater acceptance in industry over the last decade due to the efforts of a growing number of passionate practitioners who have effectively conveyed the need for a different accounting system in support of lean operations. This subject has been less than enthusiastically received in academia, perhaps due to the limited exposure in accounting to lean principles and the primary academic focus on external reporting over the information systems needed for internal decision making. Fortunately, a few academics ardently support the concepts behind lean accounting and are working to introduce this critical topic in their respective universities and in various academic and practitioner conferences. Gloria McVay, Frances Kennedy, and Rosemary Fullerton are among the academics who have been recognized for several years as strong proponents of the concepts embodied by lean accounting.

Drs. McVay, Kennedy, and Fullerton recognize the need for more educational material about lean accounting that could provide accounting professionals, academics, and students with a better understanding of the basic concepts behind it. Their various backgrounds in both academia and industry provide them with a unique combined perspective on the shortcomings of the traditional management accounting system, and the potential for providing more relevant accounting information for those pursuing a lean journey.

Dr. McVay had 16 years of corporate experience before entering academia and believes in the importance of staying current with the business environment. Both her corporate and academic focus is on management decision making and reporting. Seeing the disconnect between cost accounting textbooks and real world practices that were emerging in lean operations and lean accounting set her on a path that resulted in working with Dr. Kennedy and Dr. Fullerton to produce this book. Dr. McVay pioneered teaching lean accounting classes to university students at Winona State University. She also partners with businesses that have embraced lean accounting, giving her students the opportunity to experience real world examples. She has experience working with companies on their lean journey in both the manufacturing and healthcare sectors. Dr. McVay received the first LEI Excellence in Lean Accounting Professor Award. She also initiated faculty/student attendance at the Lean Accounting Summit. One of her students received the first LEI Excellence in Lean Accounting Student Award.

Dr. Kennedy has 13 years of experience working in both manufacturing plants and corporate headquarters. Her experience on the factory floor fueled her love for manufacturing and her quest to provide better information for decision making. Since entering academia, she has continued this focus through field research, visiting plants across the United States and Japan. During her year-long sabbatical, she was able to pour her efforts into designing a lean performance measurement system that included manufacturing, service, and project management. She is a recipient of the International Lean Six Sigma Lean Leadership Award and Lean Accounting Summit Award for Advancing Lean Education in the Classroom and Beyond. She has also received awards from the International Federation of Accounting and the Institute for Management Accounting for her contributions to lean education in the profession. Dr. Kennedy integrates lean and lean accounting concepts into the core cost accounting classes at Clemson University, emphasizing the need to understand operations to ensure that the best and most relevant information is provided to managers.

Dr. Fullerton was fortunate to have a year-long sabbatical supported by the Huntsman School of Business and the Shingo Prize at Utah State University. The focus of her sabbatical was on lean thinking and lean accounting. She worked with several companies that recognized the need for a more supportive and relevant accounting system. She spent four months assisting my division of Barry-Wehmiller in its transition to lean accounting. Dr. Fullerton was instrumental in ensuring that all accounting principles and guidelines were followed during the process. She worked with our divisional vice president of finance to encourage acceptance by the corporate team. Without her assistance, the accounting transition at our company would have been much more difficult. Much of her work was included in our coauthored Shingo Prize–winning book, *Accounting for World Class Operations*. More importantly, Dr. Fullerton used her practical knowledge to design one of the first graduate courses related to lean accounting. The activities and readings in the course are designed to give students a new perspective on internal accounting practices that, if not changed, will become increasingly distant to the needs of companies pursuing lean thinking. Dr. Fullerton has researched, published, and taught in this area for many years. She has also been involved with the Shingo Prize as an examiner for over 12 years, which has helped her understand even more clearly the deficiencies of the most current internal accounting systems. She was recently awarded the LEI Excellence in Lean Accounting Professor Award.

If you are seriously thinking about or currently pursuing your lean journey, then you will want to move your cost management practices into the 21st century in order to motivate the right behaviors and provide understandable and actionable information to the entire workforce. Anything less will leave your company with a standard costing system that is irrelevant, difficult to understand, and a potential roadblock to your lean initiatives. This book, *Accounting in the Lean Enterprise: Providing Simple, Practical, and Decision-Relevant Information*, will provide a clear, concise, and easily understandable pathway to the internal decisions so necessary for successful progress on your lean journey. Its direct and simple, yet thorough, discussion of all aspects related to lean accounting is a complement to the current related literature. It provides specific definitions of lean accounting and value stream costing, as well as discussions and examples related to inventory management, capacity management, product costing, and transaction elimination. In addition, it contains information about designing an appropriate measurement system for a lean environment that is simple, visual, relevant, and actionable. The burning question of how to make internal decisions such as product mix and in-sourcing without having individual standard product costs is also addressed. The last chapter walks you through a method for transitioning to a lean accounting system. This book should provide all of the initial information you need to consider and begin to implement a new internal reporting system that advocates, rather deters, your lean journey. Do not jeopardize your lean efforts by ignoring the critical role that accounting plays in your business.

Jerrold M. Solomon
Vice President of Operations
MarquipWardUnited, a division of Barry-Wehmiller Cos.

FUNDAMENTALS OF LEAN AS A COMPETITIVE STRATEGY

Chapter 1

Principles of Strategic Lean Thinking

Welcome to our view of the lean world. This workbook is designed to provide you with a clearer understanding of the fundamentals of the strategic lean philosophy and introduce you to methods for providing relevant, timely, and actionable information to the decision makers in a lean environment. The workbook is divided into three major parts: (1) lean as a competitive strategy, (2) the nuts and bolts of lean accounting, and (3) accounting controls and transition. Each section of the three parts will walk you carefully through the tools, activities, and philosophies of the concepts presented, as well as provide you with real-world examples and address often asked questions about lean implementations. It is our objective that upon completion of this workbook, you will be able to transition your traditional accounting system into one that is supportive of your lean environment. We believe that this improved information system will enhance your decision making, improve strategic communications, motivate correct behaviors, empower your employees, and ultimately add to your bottom line.

To give you a real-life perspective, you will be taken on the lean journey of an actual company (pseudonym Lean Manufacturer of Electrical Components (LMEC)) with specific illustrations and examples provided throughout the workbook. We are using LMEC because it is a firm that has made significant strides in its commitment to lean as a company culture. LMEC is a particularly excellent choice as an example for this workbook because it was one of the first identified companies that recognized the need to change its accounting system in support of its lean initiatives. We are especially grateful to the LMEC plant controller and managers, who have willingly invested their time and efforts in helping us to share their story—both the successes and challenges they have experienced in trying to build a lean culture.

LEAN IN ACTION 1.1: LMEC BACKGROUND

LMEC is a privately owned business founded in the early 1990s. It started as a manufacturer of electric components for large refrigeration units and has expanded into an international market. It has factories across the United States, Europe, Mexico, and Asia. LMEC has a strong commitment to quality, is ISO certified, and started its lean journey in 2004. The LMEC plant used as an example throughout this workbook is located in a rural northwestern area and was established over 40 years ago. This plant is fully committed to lean as a total business strategy. Its major customer is KKT, which is also a privately owned global business. KKT was founded in 1940 and manufactures cooling systems for large construction buildings.

This particular chapter describes a brief history of the lean philosophy and the rudiments of lean thinking. At the end of the section, you should have a better understanding of the following:

■ Lean thinking as a total business strategy.
■ Lean guiding principles and supporting tools.
■ Methods for implementing and managing lean initiatives.
■ Anticipated benefits, costs, and risks from implementing a lean business strategy.

Brief History of Lean Production

Lean as a continuous improvement business strategy is here to stay. Interest in its philosophy is creeping into every aspect of business and all types of business entities. Toyota has been the leading example of lean for nearly a half century, with an unparalleled industry performance of continuous accounting profits since 1960, supported without any layoffs (Huntzinger, 2007). However, even Toyota recognizes this as a never-ending journey, as it fought a massive recall in 2009, along with its first experience with losses during the global recession. As most people expected, it bounced back strong in 2010, and demonstrated its resiliency as it weathered through the massive Japanese tsunami that seriously affected Toyota's production for several months.

The Toyota Production System (TPS) was initially developed by Eija Toyoda after a three-month visit of Ford's River Rouge Plant. Ford was essentially a mass producer focusing on economies of scale to reduce costs. The one aspect that Ford preached, but not always practiced, and that is now a principle of lean, is continuous flow. Toyota realized that the inflexibility of mass production was not an option for its environment and focused on the concept of continuous flow. It did not have the demand for large quantities of one type of vehicle, or the warehouse space for the large amounts of inventory created by a batch-and-queue process. In order to survive, Toyota knew it must produce high-quality automobiles at a low cost with flexible operations and short lead times (Liker, 2004). With this is mind, it designed its operations around two pillars: Jidoka (built-in quality) and just-in-time (JIT) (a one-piece flow and pull system).*

Interestingly, while Toyota copied the process flow from Ford's mass production, the Big 3 U.S. automakers focused on the economies of scale approach that has been the mantra of 20th-century manufacturing (Huntzinger, 2007). Economies of scale promotes saving costs by running everything as fast and full as possible, contrary to Ohno's philosophy of producing only what can be sold and no more.† Toyota's cost minimization philosophy is to build only enough and concentrate on consumed resources, rather than produced output (Johnson and Bröms, 2000).

Lean Thinking

The objectives of a lean enterprise are to serve its customers, grow its financial status, increase its capacities, reduce its inventories, and satisfy its employees. It tries to accomplish this through five key principles:

- **Organizing around value streams.** Value streams represent the total activity and resources required to develop a family of similar products or services from initial order to customer delivery.
- **Building a production system of flow and pull.** The ideal manufacturing system is one-piece flow that allows for maximum flexibility and immediate identification of process or product errors. In other words, batch sizes should be minimized. The flow system responds only to demand from its customer, creating a pull, rather than a push, production system.
- **Focusing on customer value.** The focus of any production system should be on providing customer value, since it is the customer that keeps you in business. That means providing no more or no less than customer expectations in products, services, technology, timely deliveries, quality, and reliability.
- **Providing employees with the necessary empowerment to improve their jobs.** Those doing the work have the greatest understanding of their jobs, so they should also have the flexibility, trust, and permission to determine how to make improvements and identify problems. Your employees should be considered your greatest asset and treated accordingly.
- **Always looking for ways to improve.** The cornerstone principle of lean is to constantly strive for perfection. Realizing that the end is not attainable, you should relentlessly pursue methods for improvement.

---

* The Toyota Production System, or TPS, was initially referred to as JIT, but was later coined "lean production" in Womack et al.'s (1991) seminal book, *The Machine That Changed the World*. The term is self-defining, since lean is a method of using less of everything.

† Taiichi Ohno (1912–1990) is considered the father of the Toyota Production System (TPS). He identified the seven wastes (or *muda* in Japanese) as part of this system. He published the now classic book titled *Toyota Production System: Beyond Large-Scale Production* in 1988.

These five guiding principles create a much different environment than the batch-and-queue push systems of mass producers that concentrate on scale economies and set "good enough" objectives. Thus, in order to implement this culture-changing system, there has to be a long-term vision of achievable expectations, a strong commitment to change from the top, an unrelenting and disciplined resolve to "stay the course," and an organization-wide understanding of the need for and resulting benefits from continuous change and improvement.

There are many well-known "lean tools" that are used to implement lean principles. Some of these include kaizens, hoshin kanri, visual management, standardized work, 5S, poka-yokes, cellular manufacturing, total productive maintenance (TPM), and kanban. (For definitions of these lean practices, refer to the glossary in Appendix A.) One lean practice that is often overlooked and misunderstood, which is the focus of this handbook, is a supportive lean accounting system. All of these lean practices have their place and function in a lean implementation. But too often firms consider lean a collection of tools, rather than a total business strategy, and thus many firms cherry-pick those tools that are most easily adopted or may appear to provide the largest effect on their bottom line. Unfortunately, they are often disappointed in the results, because the individual tools are not as effective as stand-alone changes. As Johnson and Bröms (2000) suggest in their book, *Profits Beyond Measure*, too many believe the sum of the parts (individual tools) translates to the whole, which is a myth. Lean implementation success depends on the interconnectivity of using lean principles in all parts of the business.

Admittedly, some lean tools are typically more effective in leading a culture change. One of the first recognized steps of a commitment to lean implementation must start with sustaining a 5S workplace throughout the organization. Without a clean and organized work environment, it is difficult to even recognize improvements that need to be made, and it is even more difficult to sustain those improvements. 5S acts as a form of visual management, gives pride to the workers, and requires the necessary discipline to make and sustain change. Another advantage to implementing 5S early in the lean initiative is that employees learn to recognize many different forms of waste in the process. Recognizing waste (or what is often referred to as *muda* in lean environments) is a key factor when targeting improvements, and 5S is one of the easiest ways to implement and observe immediate improvements. The elements of 5S are shown below:

- **Sort:** Sort out unnecessary items and get rid of clutter.
- **Set in order:** Make a place for everything and keep everything in its place.
- **Shine:** Clean, buff, and eliminate all rubbish and dirt in the area.
- **Standardize:** Establish written standards and routines for cleaning and organizing work areas.
- **Sustain:** Use discipline and commitment to maintain order and cleanliness so 5S becomes a way of life.

> **LEAN IN ACTION 1.2: MUDA**
>
> *Muda* is a Japanese word that is commonly used. It means "waste" and refers to any type of activity that absorbs resources but creates no value. Muda is everywhere. The antidote to muda is lean thinking, because it provides a way to do more and more with less and less (see Womack and Jones, 1996, 15).

Many companies add a sixth S for safety, which should always be a number one priority. It is difficult to show respect for your employees if you do not provide them with a safe working environment. Actually, safety should be incorporated into all of the 5S elements. For a simple example of 5S, see Figure 1.1.

Another important lean tool used to support the lean pillars of continuous improvement and respect for people is kaizen events. (*Kaizen* is the Japanese term for continuous improvement.) These can range from major breakthrough, weeklong events that represent significant improvements and change, to rather simple changes that make production easier for shop floor workers. Similarly, kaizens can be formally organized or informal initiatives. Regardless of the situation, *everyone* in the organization (from top management to associates, from the accounting department to the production floor) should be encouraged to participate in some type of kaizen event (whether it is actually called that) on a fairly regular basis. Kaizens represent the commitment to continuous improvement.

Many companies have various rewards and recognitions for kaizen participation or resulting benefits received from the improvement initiatives. More importantly, the employees should consider participation in kaizens as self-rewarding, as workers are empowered to enhance their jobs from their own understanding of how to make improvements. The relevance of and desire for their input into improving their products and work environment should be clear to both them and their organization.

Lean Implementation and Management

Lean is not a faddish or quick-loss diet. It is a long-term, lifestyle commitment to change, which is never easy. If implementing lean were easy, everyone would have tried it and succeeded, which is far from the case. It is called a journey for a reason. The ultimate objective of lean (perfection) can never be achieved, so you just keep working at it a day, a week, a month, a year at a time. Many companies have experimented with lean, a few have invested in it with significant resource commitments, but only a handful have really embraced it as a cultural lifestyle.

The lean journey must certainly start at the top. Without top management commitment, it is almost impossible for a change initiative as significant as lean to succeed. As indicated earlier, organizations have to adopt lean as a total

**5s Example
Hardware Cart**

Before

After
Standardized hardware
carts—had new carts made
and labeled each part.

After
Color coded less frequently
used hardware by product and
moved to a side location.

Summary of Waste Eliminated

Sort: Sorted frequently used hardware from less frequently used hardware.

Set in order: Placed frequently used hardware in cart, and placed in order that it is used in the assembly.

Shine: Made new carts with fresh paint and discarded old carts and bins.

Standardize: Made all the hardware carts the same so stations had flexibility to all tasks required on the line; when operators flex stations, they don't spend time looking for hardware.

Sustain: Area audited monthly for compliance.

Waste eliminated:
-**Motion:** Parts are in order, so no extra movement required to find parts.
-**Inventory:** Extra parts not needed are no longer stored in the area.

Figure 1.1   5S example.

business strategy that winds its way through every aspect of the business. All employees should have exposure to and ultimately sufficient training on the concepts of lean. In order to get the necessary type of commitment to change from the workforce, workers must be reassured that lean does not put their job in jeopardy; rather, they should understand that it will strengthen their company and make their jobs more interesting and valuable to the organization. They will enjoy new responsibilities and challenges in a team environment, and have considerable input into how they do their job.

In the earlier days of lean, when it was mainly referred to as JIT, many viewed it simply as a methodology for reducing inventory. From this perspective, companies would sometimes believe that all they needed to do to "jump on the JIT bandwagon" was to minimize their inventories. This premature strategy can easily lead to disastrous problems of stock-outs and shipment delays when quality issues have not been addressed first. We are sure that you have heard your share of frightening failures from lean implementations gone awry. Thus, it is critical that a strategic plan for implementing lean is established with careful consideration of the overall effects of each change step. For some companies, major changes can be made almost immediately. But for many, lean must be done in baby steps—but with continuous progression. The most important aspect is to first sustain the improvements that have been made, and then to look for the next logical implementation sequence from a strategic perspective.

There are many different and valid methods available in the literature and in the consulting community that can assist your lean implementation. Some of the problem-solving tools that support change initiatives include value stream current and future maps, PDCA (plan, do, check, act), A3's, and DMAIC (define, measure, analyze, improve, control). You may need to experiment with various methods to find out what works best for your organization. As Jim Womack (2008) said, "Pick one, adapt it as necessary to your needs, make sure everyone understands it, and get going." A key issue is to keep management not only leading the change, but also helping to sustain it. In addition, standard work needs to be developed so that the improvements will continue regardless of any necessary changes in personnel.

Lean Results

Unfortunately, U.S. businesses tend to evaluate every change initiative by the short-term effects on the bottom line. For various reasons, savings from improving processes are often not easily traceable to overall profits. Financial statements do not have line items for improvements in productivity, inventory turns, setup times, and lead times. In fact, some of these obvious improvements actually depress earnings initially. Due to the standard costing system, when inventories are reduced, more of the fixed costs that were tied up in inventory on the balance sheet are released to the income statement, giving the misguided perception that reducing inventories is negatively affecting the financial performance of your business. As inventories stabilize, this effect will go away. One of the reasons we advocate changing the accounting system to support lean operations is to help people better understand the true financial effects from their improvements. These issues will be further explained in later chapters.

While a firm's financial statements may appear weaker initially as some of the improvement changes occur, cash flow should definitely increase as the trend for purchasing large amounts of "safety" inventory is reduced. Also, as internal processes move toward cellular manufacturing, constraint management, and one-piece flow, work-in-process inventory will become negligible. Many of the savings that companies calculate from improvement efforts are related to increased labor availability and factory capacity. Realistically, in the short- to mid-term, these are artificial savings because they are actually fixed costs that will continue. (We don't want people's jobs to be threatened due to their improvement efforts!) Unless we have a plan to use the newly created available capacity to grow our business, these savings will not provide any true monetary gains.

Another problem with calculating financial gains from improvement events is that they may be only that—events. Too often, people get excited about a project, and everyone works hard to solve a problem in the short term, and then they move on to fight other fires. Nobody stays behind to tend the solution. Standardized work is not developed. Lean leaders move on to new projects. Thus, the one-time fix is short-lived. If lean improvements are not connected across all functions in the organization, the individual efforts get lost in the total picture. However, if kaizens are done with a strategic approach in all areas of the business, if all workers have a vision of what the lean philosophy is trying to accomplish, if bringing greater value to our customers is the focus of our lean efforts, if top management is patient and has caught the vision of the lean journey, and if our measurement systems become clearer and measure our true objectives, then the culture can change, the overall profitability of the company should correspondingly soar, and market share should grow with the competitive advantages you are building. Lean is not for wimps; it takes courage, commitment, creativity, and tenacity.

As Toyota has so effectively exemplified through both its many successes and also its recent challenges, the lean journey is a learning process that never ends; in fact, as in any learning experience, the more you tackle it, the more you realize how much more needs to be done, and the harder you must work to achieve your objectives. Make your strategic commitments now, because your lean journey is too important to postpone or neglect.

Discussion Questions

1. Briefly explain the genesis of lean production.
2. What are the five key principles of lean thinking? How do these create a different environment from traditional manufacturing?
3. Identify some of the common lean tools. How do organizations sometimes misuse these tools?
4. What are some of the main benefits achieved through 5S?
5. Why might some companies get discouraged as they try to implement lean principles?
6. What are some of the most important requirements for a successful lean journey?

References

Huntzinger, J. R. 2007. *Lean cost management*. Ross Publishing, Fort Lauderdale, FL.

Johnson, H. T., and A. Bröms. 2000. *Profits beyond measure*. The Free Press, New York.

Liker, J. K. 2004. *The Toyota way*. McGraw Hill, New York.

Womack, J. P. 2008. *Lean Enterprise Institute Newsletter*, July.

Womack, J. P., and D. T. Jones. 1996. *Lean thinking*. Simon & Schuster, New York.

Womack, J. P., D. T. Jones, and D. Roos. 1991. *The machine that changed the world*. HarperCollins Publishers, New York.

Chapter 2

Value Stream Management

This chapter provides you with an overview of the organizational structure, management, problem-solving techniques, and performance measures used in a lean organization. Most of these topics will be discussed in greater detail in later chapters. These concepts all fall under the umbrella of value stream management and recognize the organizational differences between traditional and lean producers. After reading this chapter you should have a clearer understanding of the following:

- What value stream management entails.
- How to define and structure a value stream.
- How to identify problems through the use of lean tools and value stream mapping.
- What types of performance measures are used in a lean environment.

Introduction to Value Stream Management

Traditional mass producers are organized into departments and work diligently at making each department efficient and productive. Managers manage their own departments, and communication among different departments is often difficult and delayed. Rewards and promotions are generally tied to department performance, so it is natural that workers at all levels focus their efforts on optimizing their own areas. For example, production workers concentrate on quality and process improvement, engineers pride themselves in engineering development, sales and marketing focus on better advertising and sales growth, and accountants track and maintain all the costing records and variance reconciliations. In large companies, these general areas are split into several subdepartments. Then, companies will often have different departments or subdepartments compete against each other for recognition and allocation of rewards. This "silo" mentality invades all types of organizations and basically works to alienate people, create unhealthy competition, develop myopic improvements, and hamper strategic thinking. While employees in each department may be working their hardest to make their department the best possible, the macro vision of what is best for the company as a whole generally gets lost. This is especially true with the support departments. From experience, we have found that if you talk to human resource people, accountants, or even sales people working in traditional environments, they seldom visit the shop floor, and they rarely have a clear understanding of production processes. Further and unfortunately, they demonstrate minimal interest in these operations that appear to have no direct effect upon their jobs.

Lean producers have a different type of organization. They build, manage, and measure all of their operations around value streams. Cross-functional teams encourage optimizing the whole, rather than the unit. Standard departments are eliminated and evaluations are centered on the performance of value streams. This represents a major difference between traditional and lean organizations.

You may be wondering exactly what a value stream is. Value streams represent all activities and resources required to complete a product or service from start to finish. Every product or service provided for a customer should be part of a value stream. Value streams are managed by value stream leaders, who are the decision makers aided by their respective value stream members. In ideal value stream-managed organizations, all employees are assigned to an individual value stream, with the exception of a few employees who service all value streams, e.g., plant managers, human resource directors, controllers, computer specialists, and facilities managers.

Because organizing around value streams represents a major change for most firms, there is often some initial resistance to this reorganization. However, value stream management is necessary for reaping the rewards from lean initiatives. In the reorganization, it is critical to assure your people that their jobs will not be threatened or diminished. Rather, they should look forward to becoming more of a part of the company community, enjoying new challenges, and finding more job satisfaction in diverse and broader activities and interactions. Workers need to understand that value streams facilitate communication, cellular manufacturing, one-piece flow, inventory reduction, decision making, and visual management, all of which are necessary for implementing a successful lean culture.

Defining Your Value Streams

The first step in value stream management is defining your value streams. You start by focusing on what products or services you are providing to your customer that have value, and look for similarities in customers, product processes, and flow. There are different types of value streams, and you will have to decide which ones apply to your firm. The most common type is the order fulfillment value stream. Other common types include new customer acquisition, new product development, and customer development value streams. In identifying a value stream, you want to have it represent a significant portion of your business. You do not want too many value streams or to create ones that are too small. A rule of thumb is a range of 25–150 people assigned to a single value stream (Maskell et al., 2012, p. 133).

For some firms, defining their value streams is fairly straightforward. For smaller firms that produce discrete families of products with similar processes, the value streams are generally clear-cut. Most companies can easily determine their main order fulfillment value streams, but have some leftover products or services that are small or do not seem to fit with anything else. Organizing all activities into value streams may require what appear to be some awkward combinations. As is true with many types of relationships, you may find out that your initial assessment of what should constitute your value streams was not very appropriate, and you will need to make some revisions. Also, business growth or shrinkage may affect value stream organization. After some experience with value stream management, it will feel more natural and the organization will make more sense for your firm. Remember that all people and processes required to make your product or service customer-ready should be assigned to an appropriate value stream.

As much as possible, you want to avoid any allocation of resources to value streams. As indicated above, ideally all personnel and machinery can be assigned to their own single value stream. However, this often is not realistic. For example, many companies that reorganize into value streams have expensive machines that service several product lines in different value streams. These are referred to as *monuments*. In the short term, the costs of operating the monument will necessarily be allocated to those value streams that are using the services of that machine. The allocation should relate to actual usage and motivate behavior that you want changed. Also, allocation measures should be such that available capacity on the monument can be readily determined. In the long term, firms should consider how they can eliminate their monuments and replace them with right-sized equipment that better fit individual value stream products. Keep in mind that allocations are anathema to value streams, and every effort should be made to eventually eliminate as many monuments as possible.

One of the most critical and sometimes controversial aspects of value stream reorganization is assigning personnel to individual value streams. Many employees are initially uncomfortable working and being evaluated outside of their functional department. Also, former department managers may feel left out of the value stream management loops. In the reorganization, top management must be sensitive to such situations. In addition, some people may service more than one value stream—they act as labor monuments. Generally, the overlaps can be accommodated through equitable distributions. For example, if an organization has four engineers that each work fairly equally on two different value streams, two of the engineers can be allocated to one value stream and two to the other value stream—even though they are all working on both value streams. Initially, it is critical in forming the value streams to identify as clearly as possible all of the resources that directly support each value stream. Then, you may have to be somewhat creative in how you assign the costs that service more than one value stream—with the ultimate goal of eliminating all of your allocations. In setting up any necessary cost assignments, it is important to tie the assignments to the behavior you want to encourage. For example, if you are trying to reduce the footprint of a value stream, assign value stream costs per the square feet used by each value stream to encourage value stream leaders to look for ways to free up factory capacity.

As you create your value streams and assign responsibilities, it is critical to find value stream leaders who are effective, knowledgeable, and committed to your strategic objectives. Without strong leadership, your reorganization efforts are likely to fail. The same leaders who were capable department managers may not work as well in value stream leadership roles that require more broad and diversified approaches. It is also critical that your value stream leadership has a strong understanding of, commitment to, and training in the concepts of lean. Value stream leaders must be focused not only on customer value, but also on respecting their associates and enabling them to feel comfortable and confident in their new work environment.

LMEC started its value stream management by identifying four value streams. Unfortunately, the value stream leadership and multifunctional teams were not well trained in lean concepts and faced several problems, forcing LMEC to abort its first attempt at value stream management. It returned to its functional departments, but was no longer satisfied with this type of organization either. So top leadership searched for answers and led the charge. Help books were identified and assigned for management reading, consultants were contacted, and lean leaders were sent to workshops, including the first Lean Accounting Summit. LMEC reorganized again—this time around three value streams. Managers mapped their value streams, determined their shared processes, and proceeded down a much more appropriate lean path for providing customer value and service.

Problem Solving in Value Streams

Each value stream is responsible for growing its business, controlling operations, increasing customer value, developing its people, improving its products or services, increasing cash flow, and eliminating waste. One of the most widely used and basic value stream management tools for accomplishing most of these goals is value stream mapping. Value stream maps create a one-page picture of all the processes that occur in a value stream. Value stream maps have been identified as the most important tool for documenting and directing lean transformations, and represent the plan part of Deming's well-known PDCA (plan, do, check, act) approach (see Keyte and Locher, 2004). These maps provide a visual understanding of flow and the obstacles to flow and are used to help better understand processes, identify the root causes of wastes in those processes, and determine how to eliminate those wastes.

An overview of the mapping process is presented here. There are basically four steps to value stream mapping: (1) plan the logistics of the mapping, (2) develop a current state map, (3) develop a future state map, and (4) prepare an implementation plan for achieving the future state. Of course, as with all lean efforts, this process is never ending. Future state maps become current state maps, and new future states need to be created with new implementation plans.

In planning the mapping process, a team leader must be designated, along with the other team members who will participate. You will need a strong cross-sectional team that collectively has a good understanding of all of the processes from start to finish. Of course, a time, date, and location for the mapping process need to be set in advance, so that everyone involved can schedule his or her time and focus.

For the actual value stream mapping, it is necessary for the team members to first walk through all steps of the process. Each step should be timed to determine the time required for all value-added and non-value-added activities. Upon completion of the walk-through and timing exercise, the team members should draft a hand-drawn, rough sketch of all value stream activities and flow. Both information flow and material flow should be included. It is also helpful to calculate and include on the maps such items as lead times, process times, first-pass yields, and any other critical value stream measures. Use of the typical mapping icons in preparing the value stream maps will provide a common language for everyone to understand. Refer to Figure 2.1, which gives examples of general mapping icons. Figure 2.2 depicts a rather simple example of a current and future state value stream map prepared by a service organization for its accounts receivable collection process.

The real rewards from value stream mapping begin when the future state is developed—the place you would like to move to in your value stream to improve flow and eliminate waste. Before the future state value stream map can be drawn, intense brainstorming should occur among team members to discuss improvement ideas. Some of the questions you may want to consider include the following:

- What do the customers need that they are not currently receiving?
- Which current state steps create value and which ones are wasteful?
- How can we balance our workload better?
- How can we flow work with fewer interruptions?
- What process improvements are most critical?

The future state map should be as clear, complete, and definitive as possible, and depict doable objectives that can be accomplished in the fairly near future through significant efforts. You want your people to be excited about potential improvements—not discouraged over impossible objectives. Of course, everyone

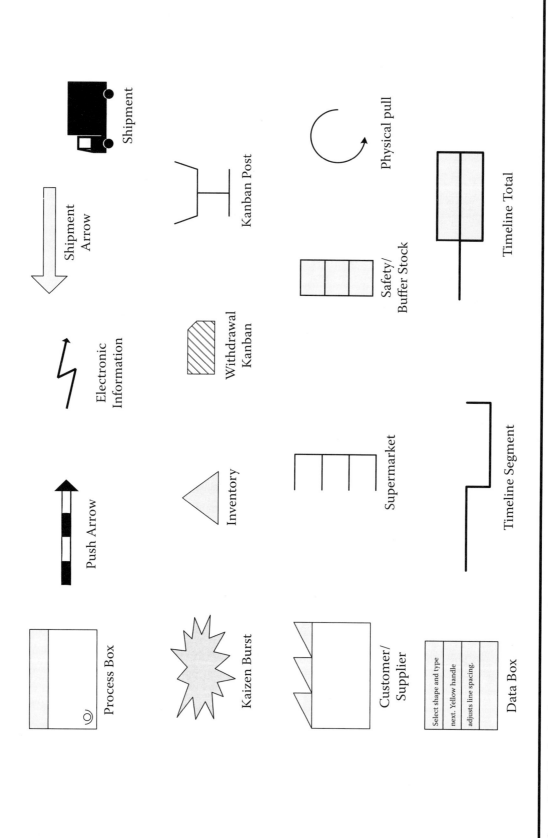

Figure 2.1 Typical value stream mapping icons.

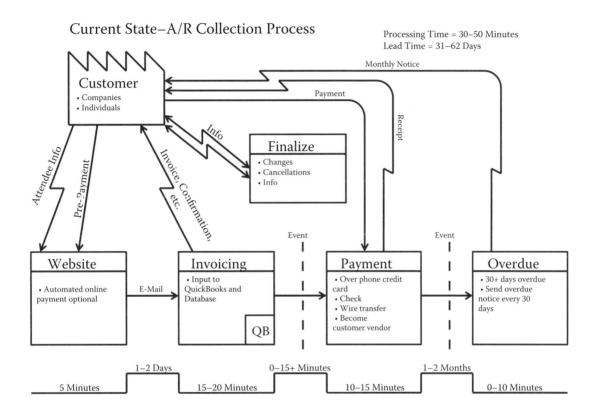

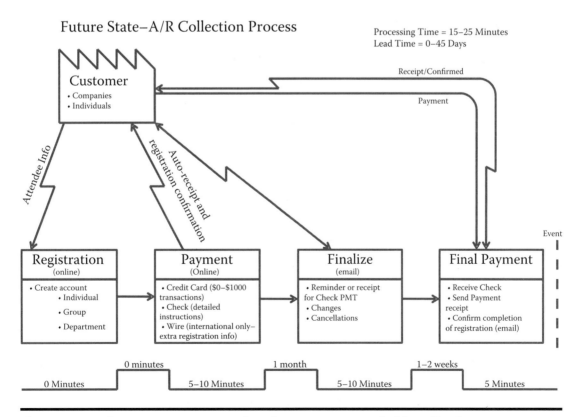

Figure 2.2 Value stream map examples of an accounts receivable collection process.

should understand that this is only an intermediate future state. Since the future continues indefinitely, so will future state revisions.

The last step of value stream mapping is preparing the implementation plan for accomplishing the future state. The main objectives expected to be achieved should be clearly defined. A master plan for achieving the objectives should be created and supported with a detailed plan outlining project review dates and responsible personnel. The plan must be presented to and approved by top management before asking for the support of all value stream members. Implementation tools should be planned and used, such as A3's and kaizens. As objectives are accomplished and changes made, the future state map should be updated to the current state, and new future state maps designed. Plans must also be put into place for assuring that improvements are sustained. Too many companies find that after the initial improvements, enthusiasm wanes. It is easy to backslide into the old, more comfortable methods. This is where strong leadership is needed for making sustainable, long-term progress.

Note: For excellent tutorials on value stream mapping, refer to the workbooks *Learning to See*, by Rother and Shook (2003), and *The Complete Lean Enterprise: Value Stream Mapping for Administrative and Office Processes*, by Keyte and Locher (2004).

Value Stream Performance Measures

When you have established your value streams and identified the personnel and costs associated with the individual value streams, you are ready to consider value stream costing. You first need to understand that the old departmental measures and standard costs are no longer relevant and will not provide the information needed either for decision making in the new environment or for evaluating improvements that are made due to lean initiatives. It will be necessary to determine what value stream metrics you want to track, report, and evaluate. Key metrics are essential for assessing whether or not you are making the improvements you want, providing your customers the value they expect, and taking advantage of growth opportunities. You will want to move your metrics out of the accounting department and onto the shop floor where they are visual and timely. Some personnel will feel uncomfortable at first as they are asked to track and evaluate their own performance. But it should not take long before they take ownership of the measures and are comfortable and even excited about reporting their results and watching their improvement.

Metrics that are typically used for evaluating value streams are both financial and nonfinancial. Some are tracked at the cell level, and some are tracked for the value stream as a whole. Overall, strategic metrics should first be determined at the enterprise level, and then cascaded down to the site, value stream, and cell levels so there is full alignment of measures. Chapter 9 goes into detail on the selection and implementation of performance measures to support a lean strategy.

As stated before, all value stream measures should be directly traceable to the value stream and to those who are responsible for and have influence over their results. If there are monuments that must be shared (especially initially) by several value streams, an assignment method should be construed that motivates desired value stream behavior, such as eliminating wasted space or buffer inventories.

Most companies start with value stream measures centered on SQDC (safety, quality, delivery, and cost). A few *key* specific metrics for each of these areas are reported to determine trends, benchmarks, and goal attainment. It is important to avoid tracking too many metrics, because that creates waste and reduces the focus of your employees. Most importantly, these metrics must be visible and updated frequently. A "box score" format for tracking key operational, capacity, and financial measures is used by many lean companies. The box scores, which are generally updated weekly with actual results, also maintain a column showing the future desired state. Many firms use nonfinancial metrics to evaluate operations along with their traditional financial measures, but very few understand and measure their capacity. Lean firms understand that improvements made from lean initiatives often relate to increased capacity—and unless capacity is used to grow business in some manner, capacity improvements do not contribute to profitability. Chapter 3 discusses box scores in more detail.

Most metrics maintained in the cells on the shop floor are updated and evaluated on a daily basis. For box scores that generally relate to the whole value stream, weekly team meetings involving all value stream members should be held to assess performance. It is important that all measures monitored are used for feedback and identification of opportunities for improvement, rather than for punitive assessments of individual worker performance.

Summary

Value stream management is a different way of managing your business. It is visual, timely, clear, and customer-focused. It opens up communication and attacks the traditional functional fiefdoms. It is supportive of lean initiatives by providing information that monitors real improvements. It helps workers better understand their operations, wasteful activities, achieved improvements, and obstacles to flow; it also empowers them to make decisions that affect their performance and job environment. It builds a team mindset that sees value in working together in conscientious improvement efforts to serve customers and eliminate waste. Value stream management is critical to the successful pursuit of building a strong lean culture.

Discussion Questions

1. How do you initially get the support of employees to embrace the value stream organization, especially for those who are most comfortable in their own departmental fiefdoms (e.g., engineers, accountants, salespersons)?

2. If you have monuments that are almost impossible to eliminate, what are some appropriate alternatives for allocating monument expenses? What are the key criteria for choosing a method of cost assignment?

3. Is it possible to maintain a departmental organization structure and still effectively implement lean? Discuss.

4. Who should be involved in value stream mapping and under what circumstances is that process most beneficial?

5. What are some effective methods for defining and managing value streams that are not a natural fit?

6. How can you effectively choose the most appropriate value stream performance measures to track?

References

Keyte, B., and D. Locher. 2004. *The complete lean enterprise: Value stream mapping for administrative and office processes.* Productivity Press, New York.

Maskell, B., B. Baggaley, and L. Grasso. 2012. *Practical lean accounting.* Productivity Press, New York.

Rother, M., and J. Shook. 2003. *Learning to see: Value-stream mapping to create value and eliminate muda.* Lean Enterprise Institute, Cambridge, MA.

NUTS AND BOLTS OF LEAN ACCOUNTING

Chapter 3

Principles of Lean Accounting

The impetus for this workbook was to discuss the need for an accounting system that is more relevant and supportive of a lean environment than the traditional costing systems used in the majority of firms today. This chapter will provide you with an overview of how that system may be formulated and implemented. While we recognize that every environment is different and there is no "one size fits all" model for everyone, there are certain principles that can be explained and followed in attempting to build a measurement system that provides more relevant and timely information to users of that information in lean environments. We will refer to this relatively new system as lean accounting (LA) for simplicity purposes. This term is somewhat confusing, since it is difficult to determine whether it is referring to the use of lean tools in the accounting department or the application of a different management accounting measurement system. While we will use these definitions of LA interchangeably, every effort will be made to clarify the connotation of the term within the context of its use.

The purpose of this chapter is to give you a broad understanding and appreciation of how accounting should be part of an overall business strategy that is built around lean principles. After reading this section, you should have a clearer comprehension of the following:

- How to better integrate the accounting area into the lean philosophy.
- Information requirements for a lean organization.
- The basic principles of lean accounting.
- Implementation strategies of lean accounting.
- Challenges of changing the accounting system.

Accounting as Part of a Total Lean Business Strategy

As addressed earlier, in order to have long-term success, firms must view lean as an overall, integrated strategic business system. Its tentacles must reach into every aspect of an organization, including the office environments of human resources, sales and marketing, and most importantly, accounting. These areas are often neglected as lean initiatives and are too narrowly focused on operations and the shop floor. However, it is impossible to build a truly lean culture without the commitment of every area in the organization. The lean journey will be slow and hazardous until it is understood and embraced by all personnel.

Accountants have a reputation for being particularly slow to respond to the call of change. They are typically risk averse and steeped in tradition. Thus, the perception by operations management is often that the accountants in general are the proverbial "bean counters" that "do their own thing" in crunching the numbers, and they are either not interested or uninformed as to the activities, processes, and decision making that occur on the shop floor. This scenario is unfortunate for both parties. Management accountants, in particular, need to understand the operations in order to provide relevant information to their customers—value stream leaders, operations managers, and engineers. Further, if they are going to be supportive of a lean environment, they should know and be practicing lean principles. Operations personnel would also benefit from the information and financial expertise supplied by accountants committed to lean thinking.

Lean Accounting vs. Accounting for Lean

Consultants and lean accounting advocates have distinguished the difference between lean accounting and accounting for lean. In this context, lean accounting refers to using lean tools in the accounting area. Certainly accounting processes such as accounts payable, accounts receivable, and payroll can benefit from waste elimination and the continuous improvement concepts found from kaizen events. For example, accountants should implement 5S in their work areas, prepare standard work for their processes, avoid batching, and concentrate on satisfying their customers. A common monthly drudgery for many companies is the closing process. How often have you heard accountants lament their month-end stress and inability to participate in other activities until after the closing process is finished, which often consumes several days at the end of every month? The burdensome closing process at the end of the fiscal year can involve weeks. There are many examples of companies that have dramatically reduced the hours required for their closing process using lean principles. (For example, see Cunningham and Fiume, 2003, Chapter 7.) LMEC reduced its closing process by more than three days by (1) making some of the standard adjusting entries during the month rather than at the end of the month, (2) simplifying inventory valuations, (3) making some recurring adjusting entries automatic, and (4) using more approximate (as opposed to exact) estimates on adjusting items that were not material.

As accountants are trained in lean principles and participate in kaizen events throughout the plant, they will gain a clearer understanding of the lean culture, be more willing to adopt it in their own activities, and more easily recognize areas for improvement. They will also have more time available to participate in critical thinking and strategic planning activities as they eliminate waste from their normal routines and free up capacity. Doing so will make them valued members of the strategic management team by engaging in more meaningful cost *management* activities, rather than spending the majority of their time on mundane issues of cost accounting and variance analysis. While the consensus opinion is that the easier part of lean accounting is adopting lean tools in the accounting area, it is also recognized as an essential first step for accountants in order to understand the methods for and necessity of taking the next, more critical step of changing an organization's reporting system and appropriately accounting for lean operations.

Traditional Cost Accounting in Lean Environments

Johnson and Kaplan were some of the first academics to openly criticize the role of traditional cost accounting methods in their seminal work *Relevance Lost*. They recognized that the manufacturing environment of the late 20th century was much different than in the early 1900s, when the current cost accounting methods were designed. One of the major differences was in the distribution of product costs. Before the influx of global competition and advanced technology, many manufacturing firms were smaller, job shop organizations producing custom-made products that involved significant labor costs and relatively minor support costs. Oftentimes, companies had the luxury of using cost-plus pricing, so the focus on cost reduction was limited. Further, since labor represented a large proportion of total product costs, using it as a cost driver to allocate insignificant overhead costs was reasonable. Accountants and managers became rooted to this full-absorption costing method that was driven by external reporting standards. As competition increased and the mix of product costs changed to where labor was relatively minor for many firms and overhead costs were more dominant with higher capital investments in technology, firms continued to depend upon their same traditional costing systems for planning and control of operations, with only minor adjustments. In fact, companies became even more focused on tracking price and quantity variances in an effort to better understand and control competitive operations. Accountants were increasingly adept at developing and reporting all types of variances. Recognizing that standard costs often were outdated and inaccurate, they even started to budget and track trends of expected variances of the variances, as explained below (see Solomon and Fullerton, 2007).

As accountants became more sophisticated in their traditional cost accounting approaches, the information they provided became less relevant and understandable to managers outside of accounting. Evidence that accountants are out of touch with their customers is provided by books and seminars developed about accounting for the nonaccountant. Amazon advertises such books as *Reading Financial Reports for Dummies.*

Besides the complexity and incomprehensibility of traditional accounting information, standard costing also violates many of the principles of lean. Standard costs were established to encourage workers to meet specific established, arbitrary standards. If they do so, everyone is pleased. Typically, there is minimal motivation to exceed those standards or to concentrate on the continuous improvement mantra of lean thinking. Some firms track dozens of different variances in a complex traditional accounting setting. Often the standards driving these variances are outdated. Many managers have indicated that their overhead standards are not revisited or changed for years. Recognizing the obsolescence of their overhead standards, but wanting to maintain trends rather than correcting the standards, these firms often budget an expected overall variance in addition to the regular individually calculated price and quantity variances. This contributes to a variance analysis system that is too complex and indecipherable. Particularly egregious in comparing actual amounts to standard amounts are any volume variances that are evaluated. Favorable volume variances are only achieved when managers produce more product than was budgeted. That means both workers and machines should avoid idle time at all costs. There is little concern about overproduction or producing only to demand. In fact, if production is limited to demand, and demand happens to be less than the original budgeted amount, an unfavorable volume variance results.

Further, as more product is produced, many of the traditional financial measures that are typically followed are enhanced, again focusing on production rather than customer demand. For example, assets increase with higher inventories because of the established accounting assumption that inventory is an asset, rather than a cost. Increasing inventory increases gross margins (and net income) due to the spreading of fixed costs over more products. Fixed costs generally constitute the majority of production costs other than materials. Increasing inventory levels moves fixed costs off of the income statement onto the balance sheet. Of course, the opposite effect is also true. As inventories are lowered with the

LEAN IN ACTION 3.1: VOLUME VARIANCE EXAMPLE

Assume that your budgeted fixed annual overhead costs were $100,000 based on a predetermined fixed overhead rate of $20 per unit and an estimated production level of 5,000 units. If your demand was only for 4,500 units, which is the amount that you actually produced, you will have an unfavorable volume variance of $10,000 (4,500*$20 – $100,000). If you produced the full 5,000 units, even though you didn't have demand for all of them, your performance would be evaluated better because your variance would be zero and you met your budget!

Table 3.1 Inventory Example

	Produce 130 Units		Produce 110 Units		Produce 100 Units	
The following represents the standard costs for your widgets: Direct materials per unit $5, Sales price per unit $25, Direct labor per unit $3, Monthly fixed costs $1,000. Assume monthly sales of 100 units and there is no beginning inventory.						
Sales	100 × 25	$2,500	100 × 25	$2,500	100 × 25	$2,500
CGS	130 × 8 + 1,000 = 2,040 2,040/130 × 100	$1,569	110 × 8 + 1,000 = $1,880 1,880/110 × 100	$1,709	100 × 8 + 1,000 = 1,800 1,800/100 × 100	$1,800
Gross profit		$931		$791		$700
Gross profit %		37.2%		31.6%		28.0%
Inventory	2,040/130 × 30	$471	1,880/110 × 10	$171		$0

implementation of lean principles, the full absorption external reporting system moves fixed inventory costs off of the balance sheet and onto the profit and loss (P&L) statement, decreasing margins and net income. If corporate and top management do not fully grasp these concepts, they will often blame the reduction in profitability on the valiant efforts of lean initiatives, spoiling the chances for successful lean implementations. For an example of these effects, refer to Table 3.1.

While the net income may initially take a hit as inventories are reduced, there should be a significant increase in cash flows—since purchases relative to sales should be correspondingly reduced. The benefits as well as the apparent negatives need to be well understood and communicated by both accountants and managers.

Standard costs are determined by adding all of the budgeted unit costs together for direct materials, direct labor, and overhead (support) costs. The most difficult part of this standard unit cost estimation is how to determine the budgeted unit price for overhead. Most companies use either a portion of labor hours/dollars or a machine hour rate to allocate overhead. Generally an overhead rate is established at the beginning of the year. For example, if a company used direct labor hours to assign overhead costs to individual products, at the beginning of the year, the total overhead costs would be estimated along with the estimated total direct labor hours. These estimates would determine the overhead rate applied throughout the year to products as direct labor hours were worked. For example, assume the following annual estimates:

Estimated annual overhead costs = $500,000
Estimated annual direct labor hours = 100,000
Predetermined overhead rate per direct labor hour worked = $500,000/100,000 = $5

Each job or product would be assigned $5 of overhead costs with each direct labor hour worked. Of course, this requires meticulous tracking of labor hours for each individual product. This method also assumes that direct labor is driving the majority of the product support costs. Decisions on product costs, product mix, expected margins, outsourcing of parts, special orders, and unusual circumstances all are dependent on these standard estimated relationships. If labor costs are minimal in comparison to material and support costs, it is highly questionable whether or not they directly affect the control of support costs. Also, if the proportion of support costs to labor hours was not estimated accurately when the rates were developed, then the product costs are not aligned. Further, most support costs are fixed in nature; yet, this method assumes they are variable and linearly driven as hours are worked. Of course, the most logical way to reduce costs under this system is to reduce labor. By getting rid of workers, you supposedly receive the benefit of reducing all of your product conversion costs. Under this system, labor is viewed as an expendable expense, in direct contrast to one of the lean pillars of respect for people. How do you motivate workers to make improvements that may result in personal job losses? How can employees become committed to a culture and environment that so cavalierly views them as expendable?

Traditional costing has so many trappings that work against lean concepts that it is no wonder most of the operations people tend to ignore the accountants and accounting reports. There continues to be a rift between the shop floor and the "ivory tower," with minimal communication as management accountants seldom have a good understanding of their customer—those working on the products and trying to make decisions on improving those products and satisfying their customers. Similarly, the operations people don't have a grasp of what the accountants are doing and how they could become valuable strategic decision makers. If lean is really a total business strategy, then it must be used in all parts of the company, and all employees should participate in improvement initiatives that further lean principles.

Lean Accounting Principles

We have spent considerable time talking about how *not* to account for lean. Now it is important to determine *how to* create an accounting system that supports lean organizations. The best place to start is to look at the principles of lean and make sure that accounting is built around and supportive of those principles. These were discussed in Chapter 1 and are reiterated here: organizing around value streams, building a production system of flow and pull, focusing on customer value, providing employees with empowerment to improve their jobs, and always looking for ways to improve.

Value Streams

Accounting related to value streams is often referred to as value stream costing—a subset of lean accounting. In fact, Chapter 4 is devoted to the specifics of value stream costing. In this chapter, we will provide you with a "helicopter view" of how it works. Accountants should assist in defining and assigning product families and their related activities to individual value streams. Their input should be valuable for determining what activities and resources are included in the value streams. One of the most difficult aspects of developing a value stream costing system is correctly assigning all of the employees that make contributions to the individual value streams. While the majority of workers may be easy to classify, there will be many that work in multiple value streams—such as engineers, sales personnel, and accountants. There are several ways to handle such situations. If you have 12 engineers that work about evenly in three different value streams, it makes sense to divide them up, so the salaries of 4 engineers are assigned to each value stream. Sometimes sales has no clear value stream connections and should be treated as either its own value stream or simply as part of the overall facility expenses that are not attributed to any value stream. Oftentimes companies have large machines that must be used by several value streams—especially in the initial formation of value streams. How do we assign the expense of these monuments? Lean accountants try to avoid allocations, but there are situations where it may be necessary to assign (allocate) monument costs to value streams. If this is the case, it is best to choose some measure that motivates the type of behavior you want in a lean environment. Most companies recognize the need to free up capacity—and thus, if it is necessary to allocate monument costs, they will often do it per the percentage of plant square footage used by the value streams. This encourages value stream leaders to focus on reducing their footprints to lower their assigned costs from the monument. This also highlights capacity and makes it visible for other costing decisions. It is necessary to understand that as capacity increases, not all of the monument costs will be allocated. Employees can sometimes be considered monuments as well—and treated similarly.

Flow and Pull

One of the clearest identifiers of a company that is truly embracing lean is that its products are moving in a continuous flow in small batches throughout the plant (ideally one piece at a time). There is minimal inventory because product is only produced if there is demand, and work-in-process is not moved in large batches waiting to be processed. There is a noticeable "pulse" to production, often referred to as *takt time*—the production time required for each process to meet customer demand. Parts inventory is supplied only as needed through a well-designed kanban system. To be helpful in this environment, accountants should be supportive of the kanbans, with information that is visible, timely, and easy to understand. They can help in the design of kanban amounts and signals that trigger inventory replenishment. If accountants are involved in the kanban design, then it is easier and faster for them to calculate inventory values at month end. They should also be providing timely and visual information on inventory trends, inventory turns, throughput times, and on-time delivery. Further, accounting information should be produced in the same lean manner as are products. There should be recognizable improvements in throughput time and on-time delivery of reports. Reports should be prepared as demanded by the customer, and the information should be no more or no less than satisfies customer demand, whoever the customer may be.

Customer Value

Accountants have two roles in providing customer value. First, they need to determine what their customer values and then provide that product in a timely and relevant manner. It appears that too often accountants just do what has always been done, rather than carefully evaluating the needs of their customers. Most of the information they prepare is historical and often obsolete by the time it is reported. Accountants seldom mingle with operations people to determine if the information they are reporting is helping with decision making. Many of the reports are not prepared in a format that all users can easily understand, and the information is often hidden in computers that have limited or difficult access. If it is necessary for accountants to interpret their information for their customers, then their customers are not being well served. Of course, accountants must always make certain that they are adhering to the rules of external reporting, and satisfying the needs of both their internal and external auditors, who are also customers.

The second aspect of customer value is helping value stream leaders determine what their customers value, and then developing a set of performance measures that help assess whether or not the value streams are properly serving their customers. Accountants should also play a pivotal role in developing an overall business strategy and then linking appropriate performance measures at each level of the organization to help assess the success of that strategy. Another key role is for accountants to help in developing an appropriate measurement method for reporting a meaningful set of both financial and nonfinancial key metrics.

LEAN IN ACTION 3.2: KANBAN

Kanban is an inventory scheduling system that supports a pull system. Designed by Toyota, it tells you what to produce, when to produce it, and how much to produce.

These metrics should be visible, updated regularly, understood by all relevant parties, measured against long-term strategic objectives, and demonstrate trends.

Employee Empowerment

One of the main reasons most companies that try to implement lean thinking do not reach the success level set by Toyota is because they cannot emulate the Toyota culture. There are probably several explanations for that struggle, but one of the most significant reasons is captured in the book *Toyota Culture: The Heart and Soul of the Toyota Way*, by Liker and Hoseus (2008). Toyota frames its methodology around a broad commitment to people, including employees, customers, suppliers, dealers, and even society at large (p. 14). In that mantra, it emphasizes a mutual trust and respect among all levels of employees. It is dedicated to maximizing both individual and team performance and challenging workers to perform at their best. Thus, Toyota is very careful in its hiring practices, and expects loyalty and responsibility from its employees in return. When associates on the shop floor have the power to stop production without recrimination upon identifying errors or defects, a sense of community and pride in their own personal growth and in their organization is established.

So how should accounting support this type of environment? Employees should be provided with relevant and actionable information that will help them better understand their job and whether or not they are succeeding. They should be able to calculate their own measures that are simple and meaningful. The measures should be available and visual to any users of that information. Workers need to be evaluated only on those areas that help them better meet their customers' expectations. Further, they should have information readily available that makes their job easier and that allows them to find ways for continually improving their team and individual performance.

Continuous Improvement

Most companies would say that they are constantly trying to improve their operations, yet many of their actions don't necessarily support that objective. As suggested above, by developing and adhering to a budget and driving operations per a set of standard prices and quantities, the message is to achieve certain targets, but there is no motivation to reach beyond those targets. A lean thinking company is driven by finding ways to improve. There is never an acceptable status quo or standard that can be met to achieve satisfaction. This continuous improvement resolve embodied in the lean culture is demanding and forward looking. Accounting should be an integral part of this dynamic environment. A traditional cost accounting system does not generally fit this situation. Trends should take the forefront, not differences between predesigned expectations and actuals. Flexibility should preclude budgets that were designed for an environment that is impossible to forecast a year in advance. Rolling targets that are updated monthly provide fluid opportunities for unfolding situations, rather than forcing production adjustments to try to achieve static historical predictions.

It is important that accountants have the training and desire to be involved with continuous improvement efforts. They will become irrelevant to operations if they don't participate in shop floor decisions. Their expertise in financial applications should be a valuable asset to value stream leaders and strategic decision makers. But if cost accountants continue to adhere to a system that people cannot understand and appears irrelevant, they will be left in their ivory towers to prepare mind-numbing, non-value-added internal reports. However, if they choose to be proactive change leaders, they will become trained in lean principles, participate in and even lead kaizen events, and take active involvement in Gemba walks. The more interesting and contributing career path seems obvious, yet many accountants are so emotionally tied to their traditional, number-crunching activities that they resist the changing and challenging opportunities awaiting them as active value stream members of a continuous improvement-driven organization.

Changing the Internal Accounting Reporting System

As iterated previously, the objectives in a lean environment for the internal reporting system are to have it simple, easy to understand, flexible, and relevant for decision making in a continuous improvement environment. Accountants are by nature often resistant to major change. They must be educated to the need for change and the expectations for their roles as critical change agents, not as extraneous number crunchers of outdated reports. Their jobs should become more creative, challenging, and value-added.

It needs to be emphasized that many of the changes suggested here for the internal reporting system are not appropriate unless firms have begun to embrace lean thinking throughout their organization. A lean accounting reporting system must start with a firm that is organized into value streams. As such, accounting for lean operations is sometimes referred to as value stream costing. This chapter introduces you to the major concepts of value stream costing. Chapter 4 discusses the details of a value stream costing system.

After value streams have been identified by product families and processes, the first step from the accountant's perspective is to develop a chart of accounts that supports each individual value stream. Every relevant cost to that value stream should be identified with the appropriate code. Assigning people to individual value streams is an important part of this process, as indicated earlier. Most of the costs will be relatively straightforward, but some people and some machines will be monuments where they serve multiple value streams. A methodology for determining where to put those costs must be devised. In value stream costing, the objective is to have the large majority of the costs identified as direct costs of that value stream. Allocations should be avoided whenever possible. Some costs that serve the entire facility (such as the plant manager, maintenance, and plant depreciation) should be maintained separately from individual product value streams.

All of the costs incurred during the period should be expensed immediately to the value stream P&L statements. After a gross value stream margin has been determined, an adjustment is made for any changes in inventory levels. As indicated above, decreases in inventory actually decrease profit margins. Thus, this effect should be highlighted, so value stream leaders are not punished for decreases in their margins created from reduced inventories—a desired lean behavior. The new reporting system should be easier for everyone in the plant to understand than the traditional format that adjusts cost of goods sold for favorable and unfavorable quantity and price variances.

As explained earlier, value stream costing deals primarily with actual costs; the standard costing system is generally turned off—especially for labor and overhead. Rather than using variances and numbers to track and control performance, the processes give visual information as to how the process is running, and trends of actual value stream costs provide performance feedback. There is no effort to categorize labor as direct labor and indirect labor, since all operations personnel are working to build the product, eliminate waste, and satisfy the customers. Maintaining individual work orders that accumulate labor and overhead costs is no longer necessary. This eliminates hundreds to thousands of transactions and frees up resources for utilization in more value-added activities. These changes also eliminate the distortions of standard costs that are relied upon as if they represent accurate product costs—even though they are created with distortions that are often outdated or unjustified. Companies whose major portion of product costs is materials often maintain a standard costing system only for materials. But this is much less cumbersome and time-consuming than a full standard costing system.

In accounting for a lean organization, annual budgets are used sparingly, if at all. A budget system that is effective for a continuous improvement firm has rolling targets that are updated and relevant to the current environment, not what was anticipated a year ago. However, it should be made clear that lean organizations do plan and forecast; they are always working toward well-defined targets and clear objectives. But these objectives are fluid, transparent, and flexible. The gamesmanship and significant resources expended on traditional budgeting should be largely eliminated and replaced with productive, current strategic forecasting and planning that is done on a monthly basis—not a year-end theatrical project.

One of the main keys to this new internal reporting system is having a relatively stable environment with low inventories. The reason for this is that inventories must be reported externally per generally accepted accounting principles (GAAP) at full absorption cost under an accrual system. A value stream costing system no longer tracks individual product costs; instead, it operates under an actual costing system that mimics an adapted cash basis system (adjusted for depreciable items in the value streams). Costs are not put onto the balance sheet as assets initially and then expensed as sold, as is common in a traditional perpetual inventory costing system. Rather, all of the costs go immediately to the income statement, and an adjustment is made at the end of the reporting period for changes to the inventory, similar to a periodic inventory system that "trues up" inventory.

For many organizations, it is not possible or reasonable to do an inventory count at the end of each reporting cycle. Further, under value stream costing, individual product costs are not maintained, so there must be a method in place to reasonably value inventory. If inventory is stable and low, there will be minimal inventory changes from period to period, so the valuation issue is relatively unimportant. Further, as inventory turns increase and the quantity of inventory decreases, inventory becomes immaterial to the financial statements, and the valuation is inconsequential for decision making and audit approval. However, it is still necessary to have an inventory valuation method in place that is satisfactory for auditor scrutiny. Since many companies continue to track materials through the system, they have a relatively accurate estimate of materials in process or in finished goods. From past history, they can generally determine an approximate rate that is related to materials for the additional conversion costs in process or in finished goods. Since conversion costs are often a minor percentage of total production costs, an estimate of these costs in a low inventory environment is perfectly adequate for determining the balance sheet inventory numbers.

If your company builds large, custom-made products that take extended periods to build, it is inevitable to have work-in-process inventory. One method for easy determination of work-in-process is to use Yamazumi boards on the shop floor that show the percentage of completion of each product. It is likely that the total cost to build the product has been predetermined, so an observation of the Yamazumi boards at the end of the reporting period can provide a simple and quick calculation of in-process inventory. For example, if you have a machine that takes 6 weeks to complete at a total cost of $500,000 and at month end it is 60% complete, you have $300,000 in inventory. A word of caution: You do need to be careful as to the rate at which product costs are incurred. Perhaps the vast majority of material costs are added at the beginning of the process, and only conversion costs are added relatively evenly during the assembly of the product. If materials represent 40% of the costs of the above example, then the in-process inventory would be $380,000 (0.4*500,000 + 0.6*300,000). These calculations fit with a lean environment; they are simple, quick, and visual.

Oftentimes, companies have various products in a value stream that require a disproportionate amount of resources that may be constrained or expensive. In these situations, it is necessary for decision-making purposes in determining product mix to identify the extra costs to build the more (less) expensive products. A cost for the constrained resources needs to be determined and the different costs for use of those resources should be assigned to individual products. Also, some products require special operations. Again, these costs should be

LEAN IN ACTION 3.3: YAMAZUMI BOARD EXAMPLE

(From Solomon, J. M., and Fullerton, R., *Accounting for World Class Operations: A Practical Guide for Providing Relevant Information in Support of the Lean Enterprise,* WCM Associates, Fort Wayne, IN, 2007.)

understood and assigned accordingly. This method is often referred to as features and characteristics costing and will be discussed in detail in Chapter 7.

All of the measures that are tracked by accountants should be highly visible, so everyone has feedback available that clearly demonstrates how their operations are performing. Performance measures should be moved out of the accountants' computers and onto the shop floor, where all decision makers have access to the information that affects their jobs. Performance measures that relate to cell activity are placed on charts by the cells. Similarly, value stream performance measures are visible and located either by the value stream or in another highly visible spot in the plant where it is convenient to meet and discuss issues and results. All of the reported measures should be aligned with the overall strategic objectives of the facility.

Companies will often report their overall performance measures in a box score format, as introduced by Maskell and Baggaley (2004). This performance reporting tool captures measures for three different areas: operations, capacity, and financial. An example is shown in Table 3.2. The box score is updated weekly, shows trends over several weeks, and maintains long-term goals. The performance measures on the box score should be limited to the few critical measures that will help achieve the company's strategic objectives. The most unusual aspect of the box score is the reporting of capacity. Most traditional companies ignore this critical aspect of their business. However, capacity determines the power the company has to grow to meet delivery schedules and produce internally. Many of the improvements from lean initiatives are focused on freeing up capacity (e.g., reduced setup times, reduced moving and handling, cross-training workers,

Table 3.2 Box Score Example

	Measures	Current	Period 1	Period 2	Period 3	Future State
Operational	On-time delivery					
	First time through					
	Average product cost					
	A/R days					
Capacity	Productive					
	Nonproductive					
	Available capacity					
Financial	Revenue					
	Value stream gross profit					
	Material cost					
	Conversion costs					

streamlining processes). These efforts do not increase the bottom line unless companies take advantage of newly available capacity to grow their business. Chapter 6 goes into detail about capacity calculations and management.

For most companies, it is a dramatic cultural change to turn off the traditional accounting system and discontinue tracking and analyzing conversion cost variances. Also, accountants and managers need reassurance that the new system is working effectively and properly valuing inventories before eliminating the old one. Thus, many companies maintain the old system and the new system simultaneously for a short period of time. Obviously, running two systems is contrary to the lean philosophy of waste, but it may be necessary until people have confidence in the effectiveness of the new reporting system.

Challenges to Implementing a Lean Accounting System

We believe that there is ample evidence available that changes to the internal reporting system are critical for a successful lean culture to develop. Yet, to date, changes in this area are progressing relatively slowly in comparison to changes on the shop floor. There are many reasons that firms maintain a traditional reporting system, but the most likely one is related to the lack of education and understanding of what is an appropriate methodology to account for lean. When the term *lean accounting* is mentioned among accounting professionals and educators, it is often dismissed as some other "flavor of the month." Also, clearly defining its properties and implementation methods is still elusive. Until its philosophy and methodology become more widely disseminated, it will continue to be received with skepticism. It needs to be clearly defined with available case studies (Kennedy and Widener, 2008) and empirical evidence (Fullerton, Kennedy, and Widener, 2013) of its potential contribution to lean adopters for more widespread implementation.

Most people will agree that the traditional internal reporting system that continues to be used by the majority of firms is inadequate, but they are still resistant to making major changes to their own accounting systems. The assumption is often that since accounting has always been done this way, it must work. Further, accountants are generally risk averse and quite traditional in their approach, so they seldom look for new and creative reporting mechanisms. Thus, besides the general resistance to change that exists in all organizations, there is also a cultural barrier to overcome in the accounting field. In addition, accountants are not accustomed to significant interaction with operations people, so they may be uncomfortable in their expanded role as more of a strategic adviser than a bean counter.

In order for accountants to be willing to change their reporting system, they must have the complete support of top management. They also must be assured and demonstrate that the new system is completely compatible with GAAP. This implies that the auditors need to be educated and supportive of any changes. In our experience, the companies that are using a lean accounting system have reported no problems in dealing with their auditors as long as they were kept appropriately informed. Most of lean accounting involves internal reporting issues; the main external reporting concern is valuation of inventories. There must be a reliable system in place for inventory valuation before reporting changes can occur. Remember that lean companies generally have minimal inventories, and the direct costing focus of lean accounting should actually result in a more accurate inventory valuation than the traditional costing system of estimated overhead allocations, with which most auditors are comfortable.

Another management concern is the potential loss of trends and comparison data from tracking budgets and standard costs. This may be an issue initially, but one that should be dismissed when management understands that the new information will be more informative, more accurate, simpler to calculate, and easier to understand.

When first presented with a lean accounting discussion and implementation proposal, most managers will initially say that these methods will not work for their firm because "their business is unique." Every business is unique and must find ways to adapt processes and concepts to fit its needs, so this explanation often represents an excuse for not pursuing a challenging improvement, rather than a valid barrier to implementation. As more companies adopt lean accounting and more examples are available for benchmarking, the assumed barriers to implementation will be more appropriately viewed as excuses, and visible changes to the internal reporting system will increasingly become more comfortable. Accountants can and should be critical facilitators in the lean journey!

Discussion Questions

1. What role should accounting have in a lean implementation?
2. Explain the difference between lean accounting and accounting for lean.
3. What are some of the reasons traditional cost accounting may hamper lean initiatives?
4. Explain why reducing inventories has a negative effect on the bottom line.
5. How can management accountants support the lean concept of flow and pull?
6. How do budgets and variances affect continuous improvement?
7. What role do accountants play in employee empowerment?
8. What are some of the major stumbling blocks in changing the internal reporting system?
9. Should lean accounting be implemented by all firms? Discuss.
10. What are some of the requirements for and differences in valuing inventory under a lean accounting system?
11. Discuss the elements in and purpose of a box score. What other ways could organizations effectively track their performance?

References

Cunningham, J. E., and O. J. Fiume. 2003. *Real numbers: Management accounting in a lean organization.* Managing Times Press, Durham, NC.

Fullerton, R. R., F. Kennedy, and S. Widener. 2013. Management accounting and control practices in a lean manufacturing environment. *Accounting, Organization, and Society* 38: 50–71.

Johnson, H. T., and R. S. Kaplan. 1987. *Relevance lost: The rise and fall of management accounting.* Harvard Business School Press, Boston.

Kennedy, F., and S. Widener. 2008. A control framework: Insights from evidence on lean accounting. *Management Accounting Research* 19(4): 301–323.

Liker, J. K., and M. Hoseus. 2008. *Toyota culture: The heart and soul of the Toyota way.* McGraw-Hill, New York.

Maskell, B., and B. Baggaley. 2004. *Practical lean accounting: A proven system for measuring and managing the lean enterprise.* Productivity Press, New York.

Solomon, J. M., and R. Fullerton. 2007. *Accounting for world class operations: A practical guide for providing relevant information in support of the lean enterprise.* WCM Associates, Fort Wayne, IN.

Chapter 4

Value Stream Costing

When designing an accounting information and costing system, it is important to consider the function it plays in providing information for both financial and managerial accounting purposes. Financial accounting reports are prepared for external parties in accordance with generally accepted accounting principles (GAAP), and their emphasis is on the past performance of the company as a whole. On the other hand, managerial and cost accounting information is designed to meet the needs of internal users, and in a lean environment, provides information by value stream as both a feedback mechanism and a planning tool for value stream teams. A properly designed value stream costing system is cost-effective, reduces wasteful transactions, and is able to serve both functions in a lean organization—external GAAP-compliant financial reporting at the enterprise level and internal management reporting at a value stream level.

Arguments made for maintaining a traditional standard cost system typically include the need to determine selling prices, analyze costs, evaluate product mix, and provide valuations for cost of goods sold and inventory accounts. But if we look more closely at these arguments, we find that they are not valid reasons for maintaining a costly system that doesn't effectively support the lean enterprise with adequate planning and decision-making information. With the exception of cost-plus contracts (as with some government and other noncompetitive contracts), selling prices are normally market driven, and not directly tied to a standard unit cost composed of *estimated* direct material, direct labor, and manufacturing overhead components. Cost distortion, particularly incremental direct labor and allocated manufacturing overhead, can impair decision making by adversely affecting management's ability to correctly analyze costs. Decision frameworks better suited to lean environments are discussed in Chapter 7.

In a lean accounting system, costs are more direct and understandable, relying on fewer estimates and allocations, and providing real-time decision-making data. As we examine the creation of value stream income statements and the valuation of inventory, it is important to note that the same accounting system used to produce internal information can also be used for financial statement creation. As we will demonstrate in Chapter 12, lean accounting produces GAAP-compliant financial accounting information needed for external cost of goods sold and inventory reporting. Of course, it also provides the relevant information needed by value stream managers to make day-to-day decisions.

Value stream financial statements are easy to understand, are usually produced on a weekly basis, and supply actionable information. Value stream costing provides the added benefit of reducing waste because data gathering is simplified. Chapter 11 identifies many of the unneeded transactions, analysis, and reports that most companies find they can do without.

This chapter will describe the underlying concepts of value stream costing and the steps needed to create value stream income statements. We continue with our example company, LMEC, as a means to demonstrate the procedures and reports described in this chapter.

At the end of this chapter, you should be able to do the following:

■ Understand the motivation for implementing value stream costing.
■ Plan and build a value stream statement.
■ Evaluate the benefits of value stream income statements.

Motivation

Value stream costing is a relatively radical method of accounting for operations, in comparison to a traditional system of standard costing, heavy inventory tracking, and variance analyses. Thus, to be successful in the transition, companies must be convinced of value stream costing's potential benefits, have value streams in place that make it feasible, be highly motivated to work through any initial challenges, and have the support of top management and the value stream teams. There are two major reasons to implement the value stream costing method:

1. **The organizational structure has changed.** Traditionally managed organizations are vertically structured with functional department managers responsible for decision making and budget accountability. Accounting reports comparing actual spending with predesigned budgets have been targeted toward these managers. Lean organizations are flatter and more horizontal. Cross-functional value stream teams are now responsible for most operational decisions. It makes sense that accounting information targets the value stream teams rather than functional departments, and supports decision making for value stream managers rather than functional managers.
2. **Controls have changed.** Traditional accounting is a transactional control system designed to collect data throughout the month, aggregate that information, and provide monthly reports to managers that "tell the story" for

the month. Through manufacturing variances and departmental expense variances, these reports highlight how closely managers operated according to expectations, and where they exceeded budgeted targets. This type of control is backward looking, focuses on outcomes, and is too late for critical decision making. Lean organizations are more focused on process controls. Value stream and cell teams want to know immediately when a process is out of control so they can make proper adjustments. They cannot afford to wait until the end of the month!

Costing Plan

In order to implement value stream costing, you need to organize your resources by value stream, formulate a plan for collecting the right information, and develop the value stream statements. This plan will guide you through the development, data collection, and delivery of your value stream statements. Table 4.1 lists the basic steps for implementing value stream costing and can be useful in devising the best plan for your company. Several of these steps, such as designing the statement format, must be completed at the facility level, since the outcome of those steps impacts all value streams. Other steps are completed at the individual value stream level, such as collection and compilation of weekly data. You will note that Table 4.1 not only summarizes these steps, but also identifies the level at which each step must be implemented. Table 4.2 elaborates Table 4.1 by breaking down the eight implementation steps into key questions to pursue that should help provide guidance to the implementation process.

Table 4.1   Eight Steps for Implementation of Value Stream Costing

Action		Value Stream	Facility
		Level	
Step 1	Identify resources consumed in the value stream.		X
Step 2	Design value stream statement format.		X
Step 3	Standardize collection of weekly data.	X	
Step 4	Compile the statements.	X	
Step 5	Select the reporting mechanism.	X	X
Step 6	Test it!	X	
Step 7	Roll up to facility statement.		X
Step 8	Obtain feedback from all statement users.	X	X

Table 4.2 Questions to Guide the Eight Steps

Step 1: Identify resources consumed in the value stream	1.1 In what value stream do the individual employees perform most of their duties? What are their responsibilities?
	1.2 How do we assign each individual employee to his or her appropriate value stream? If an employee contributes to more than one value stream, how do we share that cost?
	1.3 Can we assign all equipment to individual value streams? If we have monuments that are shared among value streams, how do we share those costs?
	1.4 Is there a procedure in place to encourage the elimination of monuments and the expansion of capacity?
	1.5 Have we identified all expenses and costs as either individual value stream or sustaining costs? Are these classifications specified in our chart of accounts?
Step 2: Design value stream statement format	2.1 Who are the primary users of the statements? What actions and decisions do they make? What key information is needed for those decisions and actions?
	2.2 How much detail is needed on the report? Do we need supporting schedules with more detail?
	2.3 What revenue categories do we need?
	2.4 What cost categories do we need?
	2.5 Is inventory identifiable by value stream? If so, should the change in inventory levels be reported by value stream or reported as a whole at the facility level?
	2.6 Are all users involved in determining their information needs?
Step 3: Standardize collection of weekly data	3.1 Who is the value stream information gathering facilitator?
	3.2 Where does each piece of information reside?
	3.3 Who is the best person to collect each piece of information?
	3.4 Have we developed and published a standardized information tracking sheet that shows the information needed, how it is calculated, how often it is collected, and who is the person responsible for collecting the data?
Step 4: Compile the statements	4.1 Do we have a simple and adequate spreadsheet to collect, calculate, and aggregate the cost information?
	4.2 Do we have a "share" drive to make one common document available to all data collectors?
	4.3 Who has final responsibility for reviewing and delivering the value stream statements?
Step 5: Select the reporting mechanism	5.1 How often will we publish the statements?
	5.2 Who should receive the information?
	5.3 Where and how should the information be posted?
	5.4 Does each user understand the cost categories, how they are calculated, and know the responsible person for collecting the data?
	5.5 Are explanations either footnoted or described on an attachment to the statement?

Table 4.2 (continued)   Questions to Guide the Eight Steps

Step 6: Test the statements	6.1 Have all value stream members and other information users participated in reviewing the reports? Have their questions and concerns been appropriately addressed? 6.2 Do the statements fulfill users' needs without information overload? 6.3 What adjustments should be made to improve decision making?
Step 7: Roll up value stream statements to facility statement	7.1 Do all value stream statements use a standardized format? 7.2 Who are the users of the facility statement? 7.3 How often should the facility statement be prepared? 7.4 What, if any, supplemental schedules should be constructed?
Step 8: Obtain feedback from all statement users	8.1 Have we asked and obtained feedback from all users? 8.2 Have we adjusted the statements for users' suggestions and needs? 8.3 Do we have a process in place for continued feedback and adjustments to information needs?

Step 1: Identify Value Stream Resources

A necessary requirement for value stream costing and one of the first steps in a lean transformation is the identification of value streams. When using lean accounting, costs are grouped into value streams rather than departments. Value streams are often identified as falling into one of the following categories: order fulfillment, demand creation (sales and marketing), or new product and business development. Order fulfillment value streams are the most common and generally defined by a group of related products that employ similar production processes. Ideally, order fulfillment value streams would include all processes, including accounting, engineering, sales, and marketing. However, sometimes these services are so shared among all of the order fulfillment value streams that they must be separated into their own value stream, as in sales and marketing, or considered as plant-wide support, as in accounting.

After identifying the value streams, resource costs can be assigned to the value streams. There are several important underlying considerations that need to be in place for value stream costing to be effective. These considerations include: (1) assigning people to value streams rather than departments, with minimal overlap among value streams; (2) minimizing shared service departments and production monuments; and (3) having production processes and inventory levels that are reasonably stable. It is critically important that the vast majority of costs are directly assigned to a value stream and that cost allocations are held to a minimum. It will likely require a significant alteration of your chart of accounts in order to make the appropriate value stream assignments.

As has been discussed previously, some employees or machines may be used in more than one value stream. These monuments are generally more prevalent

FEAR BOX 4.1: HELP! I'M LOSING CONTROL!

Initially, LMEC's upper-level managers (the functional specialists such as the site controller and raw materials manager) experienced some concern about losing control over the costs associated with the duties and responsibilities that had fallen within their department's functions prior to the formation of the value streams. But their fears were ill-founded and the new organization worked very well!

in the early stages of lean implementations. Efforts should be made to eventually eliminate machine monuments where possible. But if monument allocations are necessary, they should be created to motivate desired lean behavior, such as freeing up capacity. When employees such as engineers serve multiple value streams, it may be possible to split their costs up in an equitable fashion. For example, if six engineers service three value streams, each value stream could be assigned the costs of two of the six engineers.

A few people and related resources will typically remain outside the value streams and will be recognized as sustaining, supporting, or occupancy costs. These are costs that are not directly incurred by the value stream, but are generally deemed necessary to support the entire facility. Examples include the leaders of the functional support areas, such as finance, materials acquisition, human resources, and engineering, as well as utilities, property taxes, insurance, building depreciation, and other costs related to the plant footprint. Since the

LEAN IN ACTION 4.1: HANDLING A MONUMENT

LMEC began the lean journey with one new product development value stream and three order fulfillment value streams. The three order fulfillment value streams were later collapsed into two order fulfillment value streams by removing a shared front-end monument that was initially treated as its own value stream. The monument was comprised of four separate lines that became dedicated—two lines each—to the remaining two order fulfillment value streams. By separating and rearranging the four machines in the monument, LMEC was able to directly cost this shared process into the two remaining order fulfillment value streams that represented LMEC's two main product families. Process improvements through kaizen events eventually resulted in streamlining the enterprise into the two order fulfillment value streams and one product development value stream.

**LEAN IN ACTION 4.2: ASSIGNING
EMPLOYEES TO VALUE STREAMS**

More than 90% of LMEC's employees are assigned to value stream teams. This leaves only a small general support group at each site that consists primarily of functional specialists who work across the value stream teams to improve functional processes. For example, the materials excellence leader works to implement kanban processes (specific guidelines regarding the frequency, quantities, and logistics of parts replenishment) across the order fulfillment value streams. The site controller works with value stream accountants to implement lean accounting methods. LMEC uses a matrix organizational approach; for example, accountants are assigned to a specific value stream and their related costs are direct costs of the value stream. The value stream manager is responsible for managing all resources of the value stream, but each value stream accountant also has a reporting relationship to the financial excellence leader, the site controller.

value streams have minimal control over the costs of these resources, they are not allocated to the value streams, but instead are reported separately. There are two benefits to separating sustaining costs from the value streams. One benefit is that the costs of resources that are not directly consumed by the value stream are more visible by management, which helps to ensure they are effectively deployed. However, the primary advantage is that once these costs are separated, the value stream team can easily recognize and be accountable for only those costs they control within their value stream.

LMEC identified two order fulfillment value streams and one product development value stream. It recognized that it also had a layer of various sustaining costs that supported the operation as a whole. The company's next step was to design a statement format that clearly communicated the information, was easy for all users to understand, and contained cost categories that were meaningful to the statement users.

Step 2: Design the Value Stream Statement Format

The principles of lean accounting outlined in Chapter 3 emphasize reporting that is simple and easy to understand. It is absolutely essential to follow these principles when designing the value stream statement. Simplicity is key! Information that is confusing or incomprehensible will be either misused or ignored, often leading to inferior results. The information must be both clear and relevant.

How can you be sure that the value stream statements are clear and relevant? First, make sure you answer the following critical questions *before* designing the statements:

■ Who is going to use these statements? (Examples: value stream team, production and plant managers)
■ What actions and decisions do these users make? (Examples: capacity usage, new products, improvements to flow)
■ What is the key information that informs those actions and decisions? (Examples: space and machine utilization, value stream cost per unit, on-time delivery)

The value stream team is usually the primary user of the value stream statements. Value stream teams are comprised of employees that come from different functional areas and have varying education and experience levels. Along with engineers and production supervisors, there are also cell team leaders and material handlers. Value stream statements—as well as performance measures—contribute to the team's common understanding of the value stream's process, needs, and performance. Having mutual understanding of the value stream's performance is a very important first step when setting up action plans and developing a vision for the future state. This is what simple and easy-to-understand accounting information can bring to the table.

Once you have identified the primary information users, it is time to work through some of the details. What revenue and cost categories make sense? What format presents the clearest and most relevant information?

The main goal of the value stream team is to improve end-to-end process flow. This means managing inventory levels and flow, identifying obstacles to flow, and seeking ways of removing those obstacles. The objective is a smooth process flow, increased throughput, optimal resource usage, and improved product quality and delivery. Revenue and cost components for the value stream statements should highlight information that helps the team work toward achieving these goals.

One of the advantages of lean accounting is its recognition that different companies have different information needs. For example, cost categories in a low-volume, engineered-to-order (ETO) environment where each order is not only different but may require extensive designing before the order goes to production may vary from cost categories in a high-volume company with large orders of similar products. In addition, different value streams in the same facility may require different revenue and cost categories. For example, a research and development value stream will have very different cost categories than an order fulfillment value stream—and no revenue category at all! It is useful to maintain as many common categories as are appropriate among the various value streams in order to facilitate communication and simplify computer processing. Common categories may be broken down into more detail for clarity in targeted supporting schedules. Always keep in mind the needs of your customer; it is most important to have categories that are meaningful to the users of the information.

The value stream statement should contain the level of detail needed by the value stream team, but not include so many categories that it loses its relevance or simplicity. The following section uses LMEC's value stream statements to help demonstrate the common categories used by most companies.

Value Stream Statement Overview

Table 4.3 is an example of LMEC's facility-wide value stream statement. This aggregated income statement for the company is made up of all the value streams within the facility plus the supporting costs incurred that are outside of the value streams. This facility has two production value streams, one for mass produced products (Mass) and one for custom-made products (Custom). There is also a new products development value stream. The fourth column shows the administrative and business sustaining costs. Total plant profit is equal to the profit of the three value streams less the sustaining costs. All costs are included in the statements. The total top and bottom lines are the same as in a traditional income statement. The difference is in how the costs are accumulated and presented between revenue and net income.

Table 4.3   Facility-Wide Income Statement by Value Stream for May 2013

In Thousands of $	Mass VS	Custom VS	New Products Development VS	Sustaining Costs	Total Plant
Sales	$1,130	$3,225	$0	$0	$4,355
Material purchases	345	1,290	37		1,672
Personnel costs	228	295	152	312	987
Equipment-related costs	149	425	28		602
Occupancy costs	110	185	13	37	345
Other costs	9	15	7		31
Value stream profit before inventory changes	289	1,015	(237)	(349)	718
Total (decrease) increase in inventory	(80)	(122)			(202)
Value stream profit	209	893	(237)	(349)	516
Shipping costs				215	215
Corporate allocation				84	84
Net operating income	$209	$893	(237)	(648)	$217
ROS	18.5%	27.7%			5.0%

LEAN IN ACTION 4.3: GENERATING VALUE STREAM INCOME STATEMENTS

Our example company, LMEC, generates value stream income statements weekly and rolls up the value streams monthly to develop financial reports (see Table 4.3). Each cost must be systematically retrieved by the value stream team and supporting personnel. As we will see, the steps needed to transition from the internal value stream statements to external reports that meet the requirements of GAAP are simple and straightforward. LMEC reports that it requires minimal effort and processing time to make a few monthly adjusting journal entries that bring the aggregated value stream statements into conformance with GAAP.

LMEC has chosen five main categories of cost—materials, personnel, equipment related, occupancy, and other—for its facility-wide value stream statements. These are summary figures whose detail can be found in the worksheets of the individual value streams. Table 4.4 presents, as an example, the supporting worksheet for the mass value stream. This value stream worksheet displays prior weeks, as well as a column that accumulates month-to-date revenues and costs.

The cost of goods sold section of a traditional income statement buries the difference between beginning and ending inventory values. One common complaint is that lean improvements, such as reducing excess inventory, punish the income statement. Inventory costs, for example, are hidden in cost of goods sold, and inventory reductions without increased sales can reduce net income, sending mixed messages and thwarting lean efforts. The value stream statement makes the impact of inventory fluctuations visible by reporting value stream profit both before and after changes in inventory. This provides consistent reporting of the impact of continuous improvement in the value stream and highlights the direction of inventory changes.

Value Stream Revenue

Revenue is captured weekly through the sales and invoicing system; there are no significant changes needed from traditional reporting other than to group together the product revenue that has been assigned to each value stream. Some realignment of products may have occurred as the value streams were formed, so it is important to verify that the correct revenue is being collected for each value stream.

Value Stream Costs

The weekly value stream statement contains the value stream's material, conversion, and support costs. This statement may display several columns containing

Table 4.4 Lean Weekly P&L for the Mass Value Stream

| In Thousands of $ | Week Ending | | | | Month-to-Date |
	May 6	May 13	May 20	May 27	May 20XX
Sales	**$245**	**$328**	**$256**	**$301**	**$1,130**
Material purchase costs					
Product materials	77	92	66	81	$316
Supplies	2	3	2	3	10
Tools and tooling	6	8	0	5	19
Total material purchases	$85	$103	$68	$89	$345
Personnel costs					
Wages	$29	$32	$30	$31	$122
Salaries	14	14	14	14	56
Benefits	12	13	12	13	50
Total personnel costs	$55	$59	$56	$58	$228
Equipment-related costs					
Depreciation	$27	$27	$27	$27	$108
Repairs	12	9	9	11	41
Total equipment costs	$39	$36	$36	$38	$149
Occupancy costs					
Depreciation, insurance, taxes	$22	$22	$22	$22	$88
Repairs	7	5	6	4	22
Total occupancy cost	$29	$27	$28	$26	$110
Other VS costs					
Outside services	$1	$2	$2	$2	$7
Warranty costs	0	0	0	2	2
Total other VS costs	$1	$2	$2	$4	$9
Total costs	**$209**	**$227**	**$190**	**$215**	**$841**
VS profit before inventory change	$36	$101	$66	$86	$289
Units shipped	14,168	14,247	13,875	14,160	56,450
Average total cost/units shipped	$14.75	$15.93	$13.69	$15.18	$14.90

the current week's data plus the accumulated monthly and annual data. Some of the cost categories that are typically identified and tracked are commissions, material, freight, wages and fringe benefits, supplies, tools and tooling, depreciation, travel and entertainment, outside services, promotion and advertising, warranty expense, and allocated facilities expense. Notice that all wages and fringe benefits of the value stream are reported in total and not separated by type of labor. Table 4.4 displays weekly information for the Mass value steam. Note that each cost category contains multiple line items.

> ### LEAN IN ACTION 4.4: TRACKING MATERIAL
>
> LMEC reports the value of material received by the value stream, rather than material usage, on the weekly value stream statements. This is done to highlight the cash outlay for material each week and to track any variations from expected cost levels. LMEC tracks material purchases using a coding system that identifies raw material components by product and by value stream. Raw material cost is backflushed at standard cost upon completion of production. The standard cost of material is revised frequently on the bills of material to reflect the most current prices. At month end, an adjustment is made to the direct material cost shown on the aggregated value stream P&L statements to reflect the material cost related to the period's sales in accordance with GAAP.

Material Cost

Raw material costs are collected by value stream and reported on the weekly value stream statement according to when the material is purchased and requisitioned to the production cell. When the product is being pulled at the demand of the customer and the value steam is producing only what the customer has ordered, there is a very close match between revenue generated by the units sold and the cost of the material of those units. If a perpetual inventory system is maintained for raw materials, material costs can simply be "backflushed" at the completion point of the production process to move the perpetual inventory values from the balance sheet to the income statement. (Refer to Chapter 5 for an explanation of backflushing inventory.) Since materials are a direct and usually significant product cost, many companies continue to track materials costs in order to appropriately value cost of goods sold for GAAP-compliant profit and loss statements. Chapter 5 on valuing inventory describes the necessary adjustments.

Conversion Costs

Conversion costs on the value stream statement, which are mainly composed of fixed costs, represent the actual product costs for the period other than materials (the only truly variable cost). Labor costs are part of conversion costs and don't fluctuate on a 1:1 basis with production volume, as is often assumed in a traditional reporting system. (Chapter 7 explains this in further depth.) Total labor costs on the value stream statements are the sum of the wages and direct benefits paid to all people working in the value stream, with no distinction made for salaried and hourly workers.

According to the GAAP matching principle, all costs incurred to manufacture goods sold by a company must be recognized as an expense in the same month

LEAN IN ACTION 4.5: REPLACING VARIANCE REPORTS

At LMEC, all labor and overhead rates were zeroed out on the bills of material and LMEC stopped generating and collecting labor and overhead variance information. Like many companies, LMEC found that most of the standard cost and variance information was received too late and involved too many transactions to be of any use in improving the business. LMEC replaced end-of-month variance reports, rarely fully utilized by management, with very visual current hourly and daily operator-generated reporting that is reviewed and acted upon daily by the value stream team. This change contributed to active improvements of production processes.

as the corresponding revenue is recognized. One of the major advantages of a lean manufacturing environment is that lead times will shrink so that both the production and sale of goods generally occur in the same accounting period, allowing for the simplification of accounting reporting. Required accruals due to timing differences are minimal or unnecessary. With value stream costing, it is no longer necessary to backflush labor and overhead costs. All conversion costs are entered directly on the P&L statement as they are incurred. If a material requirements planning (MRP) system is still being used to track raw materials, labor and overhead costs can be zeroed out on the work orders, leaving only the cost of raw materials to be backflushed through the inventory accounts. Detailed labor and overhead costs are no longer needed because in most cases, costs are collected for the value stream as a whole, rather than by individual production job. This change results in significantly fewer transactions, less waste, greater accuracy, and actionable numbers that are more easily understood by the value stream team and upper management.

Facilities Cost

Another big distinction in value stream costing is how facilities costs are assigned to value streams. As we have emphasized previously, allocations are avoided as much as possible in value stream costing. But sometimes allocations are unavoidable, as in many facilities costs. When we are required to design an allocation system, we want it to encourage the optimal use of resources—that means space as well as equipment and machines. To properly motivate desired behavior and use a fair allocation scheme, we generally assign costs to each value stream according to the proportion of plant square footage it uses. The unassigned facility costs are highlighted in a separate column on the value stream statement as sustaining or supporting costs. These unassigned costs represent the square footage costs that are either administrative space or available for other operations. This cost assignment method has two implications:

- **It motivates the value stream team to reduce its footprint.** Examples may include developing ways of reducing staging areas, promoting the sale of excess finished goods, and rearranging equipment. The team knows that a reduction in square footage will increase its value stream profit immediately.
- **Plant management "sees" the cost of nonproductive capacity.** This information triggers urgent consideration of how the space can be used productively—perhaps as another production cell. There may be situations where there is no opportunity to use the freed space. One example would be a post office, where reducing the space required to process parcels and letters in the absence of increased demand doesn't necessarily mean that there is productive work to fill that space. Space usage information does, however, provide knowledge of efficient space requirements for the construction of new post office buildings.

Assigning facilities cost based on square feet used is distinctly different from the traditional allocation method where all of the overhead costs are assigned to the cost objects typically using a linear association tied to labor or machine hours. The occupancy costs in Table 4.3 that are considered sustaining contain unused production space, common areas such as meeting rooms and hallways, and administrative space. Sometimes companies differentiate by adding a line to break out "administrative." Others provide greater detail with supporting schedules. Remember that highlighting the amount and cost of space not used productively by the value stream is key for identifying growth opportunities.

Step 3: Standardize Collection of Weekly Data

Once resources and their associated costs have been identified and mapped to the appropriate value stream, a data collection routine must be established to ensure consistent and timely reporting. The first step in the process is to assign the person responsible for facilitating the data gathering each week. This person should not be required to seek out and individually compile all of the information, but should mentor the collection of data and ensure the timely compilation of reports.

Next, the source for every piece of information determined in step 1 needs to be identified. In which department is the origin of the information? Is it computer generated or collected by hand? If computer generated, do the parameters need to be checked to ensure that the data are indeed pulling from the correct source for the correct time period? Once the source is identified, an owner—the best person in a position to collect and report the data—needs to be assigned.

It is critical in developing the methodology for collecting information to establish consistent and accurate reporting controls. Constructing an information tracking sheet containing the information needed, the method of reporting or calculating the data, the timing of the collection periods, and the responsible

Table 4.5   LMEC's Standard Work for Preparing Weekly Value Stream Statements

Data Element	Method of Gathering Data	Responsibility
Units shipped	Obtained from the "Units by Week" file located in a VS metrics folder in data warehouse	Value stream leader
Value stream revenue	Obtained weekly based on query of LMEC's data warehouse	Value stream accountant
Headcount	Census of headcount is maintained on a separate worksheet updated as headcount changes are made	Value stream accountant
Materials purchased	Weekly query is run listing the materials issued to the value stream	Value stream buyer
Supplies	Logged on separate detail log as ordered to the value stream during week	Value stream buyer

person for collecting the data is a good way to standardize the process and inform all involved. LMEC's standard work for compiling value stream information is shown in Table 4.5.

Step 4: Compile the Value Stream Statements

After identifying the necessary value stream information, method for data collection, and responsible person, a mechanism needs to be established for facilitating the compilation of the data into the meaningful format that was designed in step 2. A convenient medium is to develop a spreadsheet that resides on a common drive accessible by all persons responsible for individual data. If such a drive is not available, then it is common to have all the information forwarded to the value stream information facilitator for compilation.

Facilities that have multiple value streams may find it necessary to include an accuracy control check on the spreadsheets. Remember that the total revenues and total costs for the entire facility need to equal the sum of the value stream numbers plus the sustaining costs, changes in inventories, corporate allocations, and any other items not identified specifically with a value stream. This reconciliation process should be quick and performed either in a spreadsheet or through general ledger balances.

The last compilation step is the final review and approval of the value stream statements. In most cases, an accounting manager will be responsible for validating the value stream statements.

Step 5: Select the Reporting Mechanism

Now that we have documented how to create the value stream statements, it is necessary to determine who the customers (users) of the statements are and when to publish the information. In most cases, users consist of the core value stream team and other plant-level managers, such as production and engineering. Often, the statements are posted to value stream metric boards in the plant for everyone to see. This level of transparency encourages ownership and involvement among workers.

Two other necessary decisions involve frequency and clarity. Most plants using value stream statements choose to report on a weekly basis. Where possible, this is highly desirable because there is a much closer tie between cause-and-effect decision making. A manager will remember the decisions made last week that caused the outcomes seen on weekly statements. However, when the feedback occurs only monthly, it is much more difficult for managers to associate outcomes with decisions.

It is imperative that the information on the value stream statements is understandable and clear. All items should have available clear explanations as to what is included in the figures and how the totals are calculated. These explanations may be footnoted or described on an attachment to the statement. These clarifications are particularly important when introducing the new format of the statements. *Information that is not understood is not used!*

Step 6: Test It!

Remember that the goal is to provide useful, simple, clear, and timely information that supports decision making. It is now time to see if we have been successful in achieving those objectives. Set up a time with users and solicit their feedback. Look for opportunities to improve the information. Sometimes a supporting schedule is needed or even a new line item. Or perhaps there may be more information than necessary. Be open to the users' ideas and recognize information needs that have not been addressed. Make sure that everyone understands the information and can recognize how it will benefit their decision-making process.

Step 7: Roll Up to Facility Statement

Facilities may contain one or several value streams—and the value streams may be very different (e.g., order fulfillment, new product development). Individual value streams may require different cost categories from others, which is fine. In fact, value streams are encouraged to provide whatever information is critical to their own decision-making needs. Most line items and cost categories can be rolled into more general cost categories for the combined facility statements. While individual value stream statements should have the level of detail that is beneficial for their value stream, the same level of detail is not necessary on the aggregated facility statement, since it focuses on the information needs of internal and external upper management.

LEAN IN ACTION 4.6: SIMPLIFYING THE CHART OF ACCOUNTS

LMEC changed its chart-of-accounts structure to a few value stream groupings rather than maintaining costs by traditional departments. LMEC maintains a separation of inventoried cost of sales (COS) from that of selling, general, and administrative costs (SG&A) to make end-of-month capitalization of inventoriable labor and overhead costs simple to identify.

Step 8: Obtain Feedback from All Statement Users

Now that each value stream team has provided input on its statement and those statements have been rolled into a facility-wide statement, it is time to obtain feedback from the users of the facility statement. Once again, look for opportunities to improve the usability of the information. Often, small changes in format or reporting frequency can make a sizable difference in usability. As in all continuous improvements efforts, recognize that this is an ongoing process. Encourage perpetual open communication with the value stream statement preparers and their customers.

We hope that our discussion of this eight-step value stream costing process will help you as you develop your own meaningful value stream statements. Remember that the steps and questions in Table 4.2 are only guidelines. These questions merely provide a checklist that can be used to ensure that you thoughtfully plan the statements and consider not only what they will look like, but how the data will be collected and verified and how the information will be used. Hopefully, it is evident why this value stream costing and reporting method is more efficient, less costly, more informative to all users, more relevant, and more value-added than a traditional standard costing system.

Summary

Value stream costing reduces waste because it eliminates most of the transactions associated with standard cost accounting and stops the production of monthly variance reports. It provides relevant and timely information that can be readily and reliably used in day-to-day decision making by the value stream team members. Value stream profits are typically calculated weekly and take into account all value stream costs. Most of the costs in the value stream are directly traceable to that value stream. When allocations are necessary, they are generally applied as a square footage cost for actual facility usage to motivate capacity sensitivity. The central key to implementing value stream costing is organizing and collecting enterprise costs by value stream rather than by department, and treating that value stream as a mini-business.

Discussion Questions

1. What are some of the reasons people avoid changing their management accounting system from a traditional one to a value stream costing system? Explain why you think traditional management accounting has lingered so long in lean companies.

2. How would value stream costing better support a lean manufacturing firm? What would be the most obvious motivation for your company to change its internal financial reporting system?

3. What is the first process that should be done in implementing value stream costing? What are some of the major challenges that you might find in organizing a value stream costing system?

4. Discuss the main differences between a value stream P&L and a traditional P&L. How does a value stream P&L improve decision making?

5. Why is it important to set up standard work for preparing the value stream P&L?

6. How often should the value stream statements be published? Who participates in preparing the value stream statements? How do you determine who the users of the information are?

7. What information is found on the facility P&L value stream statement that is not found on the individual value stream P&L statements? What information is found on the individual value stream P&L that may not be found on the facility P&L?

Chapter 5

Inventory Management

As your company moves from traditional thinking and batch processing to lean thinking and one-piece flow, you will find that a lean business management system is needed to accurately convey the impact of lean improvements. As stated earlier, traditional standard cost systems result in financial statements that disguise the improvements achieved from continuous improvement. In fact, the profit and loss (P&L) often initially shows degradation in profits due in large part to reduced inventory levels. Without a better accounting system for identifying the gains achieved as a result of lean methods, upper management may question the advisability of continuing the lean journey. Lean accounting isolates the effects of inventory changes on the P&L at a company-wide level, and because it makes operational improvements and capacity gains achieved from process improvement efforts more visible, upper management will be able to better assess the benefits from lean initiatives.

When lean principles were first introduced in the United States, a primary focus was on reducing inventory through just-in-time (JIT) practices. Even though lean is now defined much more broadly than JIT, inventory management and reduction remain a very important part of lean operations. Accounting plays a critical part in the mix since it is responsible for reporting inventory values to both internal and external users. Unfortunately, traditional accounting systems often provide misleading information related to product costs and inventory that often encourages antilean behaviors. Companies must be educated about these reporting distortions, especially as they are trying to effectively implement lean and reduce inventories. Lean accounting methods support lean transitions with more relevant, streamlined, user-friendly information.

This chapter will work to unmask the issues of inventory valuation, and discuss the transition from a traditional costing system to the use of lean accounting methods. It will also suggest useful metrics for monitoring and managing inventory levels. When you finish this chapter, you should have a better understanding of the following:

- The challenges presented by using a standard costing system in a lean environment.
- Lean accounting methods for valuing inventory.
- Transitional steps from standard cost to lean valuation of inventory.

Inventory Valuation under a Traditional Standard Costing System

As discussed in Chapter 3, a traditional standard cost system is transaction-intensive because of the necessity of tracking large amounts of discrete inventory items through the production cycle. Standard costs used to value inventories and make product-related decisions are based on annual predetermined estimates for direct material, direct labor, and manufacturing overhead. Two particularly vexing problems embedded in a standard costing system are: (1) the treatment of direct labor as a variable cost that fluctuates in direct proportion to units produced; and (2) the usage of a predetermined manufacturing overhead rate that is based on a linear cost driver, such as machine hours or labor hours/dollars. In reality, labor is generally a fixed cost in the short term, with the exception of temporary workers, and the majority of manufacturing overhead costs are also fixed and often have no direct relationship to labor costs. So for many decisions, treating these conversion costs as relevant, variable costs is misleading.

Another problem related to a standard costing system is its focus on the variances created from the differences between actual and standard costs. As each unit is produced, it is assigned its corresponding full standard cost (or accumulated standard cost of components if the units are in work-in-process (WIP)). Standard costs are tracked through the production system through the use of the standard bill of materials and routings. Actual product costs are recorded separately. The differences between standard and actual product costs are evaluated at the end of a reporting period, usually monthly, and result in price and quantity variances for material and labor, as well as spending and volume variances for manufacturing overhead. The variances are typically expensed on the P&L statement: increasing (decreasing) cost of goods sold (COGS) when actual costs are higher (lower) than standard costs. Favorable variances (actual costs are lower than standard costs) are generally considered good, and vice versa. However, focusing on improving variances can motivate nonlean behaviors, such as buying large quantities of raw materials to take advantage of quantity discounts that improve price variances, or building finished goods inventory that absorbs manufacturing overhead and enhances volume variances. Variance analysis also encourages departments in a traditional company to optimize the performance of their individual departments, rather than concentrating on customer value and the long-term profitability of the company as a whole.

Although most people understand that achieving a certain profit margin is critical—many do not understand how that margin is actually calculated. Gross margins are the result of net sales minus cost of goods sold. Cost of goods sold is a function initially of all standard product costs incurred in the period adjusted by changes in inventory levels. This figure is further adjusted by the price and quantity variances of materials, labor, and overhead to get to the reported cost of goods sold and resulting gross margin. Individual actual costs for material, labor, and specific overhead items are not transparent on the financial statements, since these are all lumped into a single operative cost of goods sold figure that provides minimal actionable information. As shown in Chapter 3, increasing inventory, which is contrary to desired lean behavior, can actually increase profit margins by moving product costs from the P&L to the balance sheet.

Inventory Valuation Using Lean Accounting Methods

As lean production processes are introduced and begin to mature in an organization, inventory levels will likely drop substantially and inventory will come under visual control using lean inventory management methods, such as kanban systems. More stable and lower inventory levels allow companies to consider turning off their standard costing systems. However, this is understandably a frightening thought to many people, as they contemplate the following critical question: *How do we value inventory and cost of goods sold without standard costs for our products?* In addition, they may wonder if they can comply with generally accepted accounting principles (GAAP) and satisfy their external auditors with a system that no longer tracks inventory. Rest assured that the lean accounting methods described here will fully satisfy both the auditors and GAAP. Those companies that have transitioned from their standard costing system to lean accounting methods report no problems with their auditors as long as the auditors are kept informed of the change process. Remember that with lower and more stable inventories, there is minimal financial risk of inaccurately valuing inventories on the balance sheet and the corresponding cost of goods sold on the P&L. Further, decision makers find that having individual product costs (that are likely inaccurate anyway) is not as important as understanding the *relevant* costs that affect the value stream margins. The rewards for firms implementing value stream and lean accounting systems are inventory valuation methods that reduce reliance on complex computer tracking systems and lighten workloads for operations and finance.

One of the main objectives of a lean accounting system is to eliminate the many transactions involved in inventory tracking. In a perfect lean accounting world—where one-piece flow exists, cycle times are short, and inventory is minimal—raw material costs could be expensed as purchased, conversion costs could be expensed as incurred, and the value of finished goods would be recorded as cost of goods sold at the point of transfer of ownership to the purchaser. There would be no need for detailed tracking of material, labor, and manufacturing overhead to individual units of production.

FEAR BOX 5.1: VALUING INVENTORY

"How do we value inventory and cost of goods sold if we don't use standard costs for our products? Doesn't GAAP require us to use standard costs?"

GAAP requires a fair valuation of inventory—one that accurately reflects its value without materially overstating or understating the balance sheet. It does not require standard costing. LMEC reports no issues with GAAP requirements. It has continued to receive unqualified audit opinions with inventory balances calculated as demonstrated in our example. However, to avoid any audit issues, your auditors should be involved early in the change process from a traditional to a lean accounting system. Many CPA firms have now trained their employees to be proficient in the audit of companies using lean accounting.

More realistically, companies begin simplifying inventory tracking by first eliminating the detailed tracking of conversion costs (labor and overhead). This significantly reduces transaction reporting and other wastes that occur in maintaining detailed inventory records. Fully burdened standard costs no longer exist, and product costs are averages of actual value stream costs—not tracked and determined individually. Any inventory tracking is generally from a material content perspective only, with adjustments for ending inventory conversion costs added at the end of the reporting period to material inventories. Such a system requires a company to maintain raw material standard costs based on detailed bills of material, and tracks the materials from ordering through the sale of finished goods. All labor and overhead costs of the period are charged directly to the value streams. As demonstrated in Chapter 4, value stream P&Ls contain *actual* (not standard and allocated) labor and overhead costs of the period. Thus, the value stream product costs should in fact be more accurate than those of the traditional costing system with their arbitrary overhead allocations. Either at the value stream or aggregated level, a calculation is made monthly to capitalize the appropriate inventoriable conversion costs, which will bring the enterprise-level P&L into alignment with GAAP. This approach is similar to the inventory valuation method used by our example company, LMEC. It is important to note that valuing inventory for a lean enterprise is *not* comparable to a traditional periodic system of adding up all of the individual product costs of units that have not been sold and adjusting the inventory accounts accordingly. Nor is it a traditional perpetual system where all product costs are initially entered into the inventory asset account and then moved onto the income statement as the products are sold. It is more a macro, hybrid perspective of moving any period changes in inventory levels for conversion costs from the P&L statement to the balance sheet for increases in inventories, and vice versa for decreases. Most firms maintain material costs on a perpetual basis, so the financial statements reflect accurate material product costs and no ending period adjustments are necessary.

Conversion Costs Inventory Evaluation. A challenge for firms transitioning to lean accounting is to determine exactly how they will calculate the end-of-period inventory adjustment for conversion costs. There are various approaches that can be taken. Similar to many companies, LMEC records its materials costs such that the ending inventory is maintained on the balance sheet. To determine ending labor and overhead inventory, it uses a macro valuation method based on an average daily conversion cost times the estimated number of days of materials inventory on hand at the end of the month. This is a simple calculation that is straightforward and easy to understand and maintain. The inventory conversion costs are moved from (to) a P&L expense account to (from) a balance sheet asset account according to increases (decreases) in the days of inventory on hand. The change in the inventory conversion costs is added to the standard raw material costs to "true up" the ending inventory. A simple example of this approach is shown in Figure 5.1.

LMEC calculates a single-site-level inventory figure, instead of determining the inventory for each value stream. Other firms may prefer to calculate the inventories for their individual value streams. It may be easier to get the relevant relationships for the conversion costs if it is done on a smaller value stream-level scale. In addition, showing the change in inventories for individual value streams may motivate better value stream inventory management. On the other hand, some companies may find no benefit in determining

---

1. Calculate the number of days of inventory in raw materials.
   20 Days

2. Calculate the conversion costs to be inventoried by taking the number of days of inventory times the average daily conversion cost.

   Monthly conversion costs = $90,000; $90,000/30 = $3,000 per day; $3,000 * 20 days = $60,000

3. Make the adjustment to the inventory account for changes in conversion costs inventory.
   Assume the conversion costs beginning inventory is $80,000

   $80,000 – $60,000 = $20,000 (decrease inventory, increase cost of goods sold, and decrease profit by this amount).

4. Calculate the total inventory costs.

Raw materials inventory	$200,000
Conversion costs beginning inventory	$ 80,000
Less conversion cost decrease in inventory	$<20,000>
Ending total inventory	$260,000

Figure 5.1   A simple approach to valuing inventory.

individual value stream inventories for each reporting period, and prefer the more simple plant-wide adjustment.

Another simplified version for estimating ending inventory values is to first determine from historical numbers an appropriate percentage for conversion costs relative to materials; then add that percentage of conversion costs to the materials inventory. This approach assumes that the relationships between raw materials and conversion costs are relatively stable and that raw materials represent a significant portion of total product costs. For example, assume that previous annual trend history has demonstrated a finished goods inventory materials-to-conversion costs ratio of 4:1. Thus, if you were still tracking materials and knew that your ending finished goods materials inventory was $400,000, you would add another $100,000 to that figure for conversion costs to determine your total ending inventory.

Job Shop Inventory Valuation. There are many job shop manufacturing firms that build products with a longer production time, and thus have significant amounts of work-in-process even though they may be practicing lean. These companies will often use Yamazumi boards to track their production. Yamazumi boards were introduced in Chapter 3. They are visual representations on the shop floor of the work schedule and the percentage of complete for work-in-process. These boards are most applicable for complex assembly operations that require longer build cycles. The standard build process for each cell is posted on a Yamazumi board. The standard work for each segment of the process is listed on the board, and as each activity is completed, it is indicated on the board. This provides clear visibility as to the status of each machine build; it also guides balancing of the workload. As a secondary benefit, the Yamazumi boards allow for a simple valuation of ending work-in-process inventory by providing the percentage complete of each machine. The total conversion costs for the machine are generally predetermined prior to the build process as part of the bidding process. Thus, the value of the work-in-process would be the percentage complete shown on the Yamazumi board at the end of the reporting period times the forecasted conversion costs for the machine (Figure 3.2 shows an example of an actual Yamazumi board).

Here is an example of the Yamazumi board approach for determining the cost of ending inventory. Assume you have two machines in process. Machine 1 is 40% complete and machine 2 is 70% complete at the end of the period. Machine 1 is expected to have a total of $300,000 conversion costs, along with $1,000,000 of materials. Machine 2 is expected to have $200,000 of conversion costs, along with $700,000 of materials. For simplicity, assume that all of the materials costs are incurred at the beginning of the process and the conversion costs are added evenly throughout the process, which approximates a reasonable cost pattern for large assembly operations. Ending WIP would be calculated as follows:

Machine 1: $1,000,000 + (0.4 × $300,000) = $1,120,000
Machine 2: $700,000 + (0.7 × $200,000) = 840,000
Total WIP inventory: $1,960,000

Calculating this inventory value would take only a few minutes of an accountant's time on the shop floor. This method would have the added benefit of getting the accountant more informed and involved with the operations people.

These are obviously very simple inventory valuation examples, but the overall concepts should be adaptable to your operations. The main idea is to simplify the inventory valuation by eliminating labor tracking and individual worksheets. However, it is critical to understand that inventories have to be stable and relatively low for this to work. When inventories do not fluctuate very much from one period to another, there is little risk of a material misstatement of inventory valuation for GAAP purposes. Even with that caveat in mind, if you have approached your inventory valuation correctly and reasonably using accounting for lean concepts, your inventory valuation should actually be more accurate than with traditional methods replete with overhead allocations from standard cost rates arbitrarily tied to labor or machine hours. Unfortunately, even though companies may understand that there are deficiencies in the traditional accounting system, they generally remain resistant to change and are more comfortable with the methods they have been using for years, regardless of their accuracy.

Transitioning to an Accounting for Lean System

Lean is a maturity process and changes to the inventory valuation system must normally proceed with caution and according to the level of lean adoption. In the early stages of lean adoption, one of the most important goals is process stabilization. The focus should be on 5S and standardizing work so that irregularities in the process flow become visible. It is also important to identify bottlenecks. Too many lean neophytes have the impression that to adopt lean simply means to immediately reduce inventories. Failures and horror stories abound with this approach. Inventory reduction is an *outcome* associated with waste reduction and flow—it is not a goal. Inventory levels cannot be dramatically reduced before addressing other production obstacles first. Reducing inventory too soon could mean starving processes downstream from a bottleneck. It is actually necessary to provide a buffer of inventory around bottleneck problems, and traditional costing systems may be adequate until processes are stabilized and inventories are relatively low.

Similar to the lean journey, changing to a lean accounting system is generally a gradual process. As inventories are reduced, bills of material become more accurate, and a systematic method for recording scrap is implemented, some companies will transition first to a backflushing system to maintain perpetual inventory balances. Backflushing uses a modified standard costing system, generally eliminating the tracking of WIP conversion costs through the production system. When goods are completed, they are recorded as finished goods at standard costs. Variances between standard and actual costs are still calculated and cost of goods sold is adjusted accordingly. Backflush costing can be an effective interim method for valuing inventory, since this system does reduce some of the wasteful inventory tracking and transaction reporting. A brief overview of backflush costing is provided in the appendix at the end of this chapter.

Besides having stable inventories, there are other critical lean practices that should be in place before a major change in the accounting system is made. Companies should be organized into value streams. Pull systems and kanbans should be established to bring inventory levels under visual control. Raw materials should be delivered frequently in small batches to the point of use, where they are stored in small amounts that are easily monitored with a visual system. Kanban systems are established with standardized amounts of work-in-process (SWIP) clearly delineated by visual markings that allow for quick identification of actual work-in-process variations. Standardized work to help stabilize processes should be well defined. (For a more detailed description of the lean maturity path required before the standard costing system can be shut off, refer to *Practical Lean Accounting* (Maskell et al., 2012).) Companies will often transition away from a standard cost system in stages, taking an intermediate step or even running parallel systems for a relatively short period of time until they are comfortable with the accuracy and effectiveness of the new system. A more complete explanation of the actual accounting transition process for a lean enterprise is provided in Chapter 12.

Monitoring of Inventory Levels

Current assets, such as inventory and accounts receivable, are a necessary part of business but represent "waiting" for cash investments to return cash profits. As depicted earlier, reducing inventories can often result in lower profit margins. However, direct financial benefits from reducing inventory do occur through increased cash flows. As you lower your cash investment in inventory, the collection cycle is shortened, freeing up cash to take advantage of other growth opportunities. In this way, our investment in waiting assets (waiting to use raw material, waiting to complete and sell finished goods, and waiting to collect cash from our customers) is reduced by productively deploying our additional cash flows garnered from lower inventory purchases.

There are several common metrics that can be followed and used to measure effective inventory management. Some of these include the actual dollar value of inventory, inventory as a percentage of total assets, days of inventory on hand, and inventory turns. The dollar value of inventory shows the amount of resources tied up in inventory. This amount can also easily be evaluated as a percentage of total assets, which helps put into perspective the levels of inventory in relationship to any growth or shrinkage that your firm may be experiencing. However, keying on inventory levels in either absolute form or as a ratio of total assets fails to provide context of inventory levels versus customer demand for your products. Thus, these measures should be used in conjunction with inventory metrics that track the actual usage of inventory compared to demand, as captured in days of inventory on hand and inventory turns.

Inventory turns is a straightforward measure that is tracked by most firms. Stated in its most simple and common form, inventory turns is the result of dividing cost of goods sold (the total of raw materials, labor, and overhead for the units sold) by average total inventory. For example, if your cost for products sold during a period is $360,000 and your average inventory is $30,000, you have 12 inventory turns (360,000/30,000). Lower inventory turns are an indicator of possible overproduction, which leads to many other wastes. Of course, the more inventory turns you have, the better off you are, since this indicates the pace at which you are satisfying customer demand and ultimately turning a profit on your product. Additionally, the higher your inventory turns, the lower your inventory levels are, and the less valuation risk there is involved in switching to a lean accounting system. So this is a critical metric to track for any firm on a lean journey. Days-of-inventory on hand is a simple extension of inventory turns. Per the above example, if you have 12 inventory turns a year, you are averaging 30 days of inventory on hand (assuming 360 days in a year). Companies sometimes prefer reporting days of inventory over inventory turns because it is easier for most people to understand.

For more in-depth analysis, some firms may break down their inventory metrics into their various elements, e.g., raw materials, work-in-process, and finished goods. They also may want to track the inventory metrics separately for materials and conversion costs. If raw materials are the driving product cost for a company, inventory management metrics may be focused solely on materials, which is the approach that LMEC uses. The most important characteristics of any monitored metrics are that they are simple to calculate, easy to understand, consistently measured, and useful for decision makers.

LEAN IN ACTION 5.1: CHANGING ROLE OF BUYERS

Since adopting lean practices, the buyers at LMEC have become responsible for inventory levels. Prior to lean, a buyer's main concern was just getting materials, not worrying about inventory levels. LMEC's buyers would order in large quantities to take advantage of discounts. What LMEC has learned is that long-term contracts with suppliers offer the same discount but delivery is in smaller quantities. The value stream perspective of costs and flow removes the previous narrow view of optimizing the purchasing function by focusing primarily on price. Better buying decisions plus increased operational flow have resulted in significant gains for the company—inventory turns have increased, days-of-inventory has decreased, and dock-to-dock time has decreased.

Summary

Every manufacturing firm is concerned about managing and valuing its inventory. Two of the most common benefits to firms that embrace the lean philosophy are reduced inventory levels and more stable processes. Unfortunately, the traditional accounting system does not effectively support these activities. In fact, a traditional standard costing system may actually be detrimental to a lean transition, since reducing inventories often leads to lower profit margins and negative variances. Although a lean accounting system does not change how lower inventory levels affect income, it does highlight the inventory changes on the P&L so managers can better understand why they may be experiencing lower profitability while successfully reducing inventories. A traditional accounting system is also filled with tracking and transaction waste. Firms that have taken significant steps along their lean journey should consider transitioning their standard costing system to a lean accounting system to more efficiently value and manage their inventories. By concentrating on actual costs and value stream margins, people can focus more on delivering customer value and using relevant costs to make decisions. Inventory can be valued at the end of a reporting period using simple methods that no longer require extensive, complex tracking systems. Accounting resources can then be used for more productive strategic management decision making rather than on non-value-added, complex inventory tracking systems.

Appendix: Primer on Backflush Costing

Traditional costing systems use sequential tracking of costs, where journal entries are recorded as costs flow through the purchasing cycle, the production cycle, the completion of finished goods, and the sale of finished goods. An alternative approach to sequential costing is backflush costing. Backflush costing is a simplified inventory system that avoids many of the transactions involved in a sequential tracking system. It uses *trigger points* to "flush out" (record) the costs of inventory based on standard costs. Variances from standard costs are recognized and typically closed to cost to goods sold. Backflush costing normally eliminates work-in-process inventory as a trigger point. This is a reasonable approach in low-inventory environments where work-in-process inventory is minimal because of very short cycle times and one-piece flow.

There are several variations to backflush costing depending on the number and placement of trigger points that are used to flush out costs. There are generally three potential trigger points for journal entries: (1) the purchase of raw material and incurring of conversion costs, (2) the completion of finished goods, and (3) the sale of finished goods. We will illustrate the use of three trigger points, but there are variations to backflush costing that use two rather than three trigger points. Our example refers to two types of product costs: direct materials and conversion costs.

1. First trigger point: The purchase of raw material is debited at actual cost. The difference between standard cost and actual cost is journalized to COGS at the end of the month. This brings the raw material inventory account to standard cost. Conversion costs are recorded at actual cost.

Journal entry:	
Raw material control	$ actual cost
Accounts payable control	$ actual cost

Journal entry:	
Conversion cost control	$ actual cost
Various accounts	$ actual cost

Note: LMEC has an intermediate trigger point when sub-assemblies are completed, relieving raw material at standard cost based on the bill of materials. Companies using backflush costing often omit this trigger at work-in-process, especially if inventory levels are low and stable.

2. Second trigger point: Finished goods are completed. The standard cost of raw materials is flushed out at this point with a credit to raw materials for the standard costs of raw materials (based on the bill of materials) and a debit to finished goods.

Journal entry:	
Finished goods inventory	$ standard material cost of finished units
Finished goods inventory	$ standard conversion cost of finished units
Raw material inventory	$ standard material cost of finished units
Conversion cost control	$ standard conversion cost of finished units

3. Third trigger point: Units are sold. Finished goods inventory is relieved at standard cost. Cost of goods sold is recognized. A month-end entry is also made to close out the raw materials and conversion control accounts. The ending balances are moved to cost of goods sold, with ending debit balances increasing COGS, and ending credit balances decreasing COGS.

Journal entry:	
Cost of goods sold	$ standard cost of units sold
Finished goods inventory	$ standard cost of units sold

Of course, this example of a backflush costing system can only be used if the WIP inventories are immaterial. Companies that do not maintain material amounts of finished goods inventory may use only two trigger points, and the standard product costs would be debited directly to cost of goods sold instead of finished goods. If this is the case, however, one would encourage a company to consider eliminating its standard costs and backflush costing system in favor of a pure lean accounting system that uses only actual costs and adjusts for changes in inventory levels at the end of the period.

Discussion Questions

1. From an inventory valuation perspective, what are some of the reasons that a traditional standard costing system is not effective for a lean company?
2. Why are companies resistant to changing their internal accounting system?
3. Under what circumstances should companies consider transitioning to a lean accounting system? What problems should they anticipate in the transition period?
4. How can companies value their inventory meeting GAAP requirements without a standard costing system?
5. What are some of the benefits of eliminating a standard costing system?
6. What is a Yamazumi board and how can it be used to value work-in-process inventory?
7. What is a backflush costing system and when should it be used?

Reference

Maskell, B., B. Baggaley, and L. Grasso. 2012. *Practical lean accounting.* Productivity Press, New York.

Chapter 6

Capacity Management

Knowing what your customer values and then fulfilling customer demand on a pull basis are fundamental to lean thinking. To answer customer demand, you must have the capacity to produce at customer takt time (the rate of customer demand). As suggested in Chapter 3, a key motivation driving lean initiatives is to free up capacity that can then be used to grow the business. Thus, measuring, recognizing, and managing capacity is a critical business management issue.

Lean companies are organized and managed at the cell and value stream levels. Capacity management allows us to understand and improve the overall ability of the value stream to deliver products or services. But in order to optimize the value stream, you must first understand cell operations, since that is the level where bottlenecks and uneven flows can be uncovered. The cell details allow us to better understand the flow of processes required to deliver our product or service to our customers.

In Chapter 4, we introduced you to several different types of value streams (e.g., order fulfillment, new product development, sales and marketing). To demonstrate the principles of capacity management, this chapter focuses primarily on the order fulfillment value stream, which includes all of the people, machines, and space that enable the production processes to occur. At the end of this chapter you should be able to do the following:

- Recognize the need for careful capacity management in a lean environment.
- Understand how to develop and record capacity measures.
- Use capacity measures to identify bottleneck (constraint) cells in your value streams.
- Analyze the results of kaizen improvements on available capacity.
- Understand the value of capacity measures as a means to measuring lean improvements.

Capacity Management—An Overview

An important lesson of the lean journey is that significant operational improvements resulting from kaizen, continuous improvement, and just-do-it activities may not deliver an immediate or direct impact on the financial performance of the company. In fact (as discussed in Chapter 5), reducing excess inventory may actually create a negative impact on the P&L. However, the box score capacity measures can counter that negative perception of lean initiatives by revealing how eliminating process waste improves available capacity. Of course, increased capacity is only a benefit if it is identified and visual so that decisions can be made to use it productively.

Chapter 3 introduced the box score as a fundamental management and decision-making tool for lean companies. The box score provides a three-dimensional view of the value stream: (1) operational performance, (2) capacity usage and availability, and (3) financial performance. Box score data for operational performance are collected and maintained on value stream visual management boards, and the financial performance information is generally obtained from value stream P&Ls and supporting schedules. Capacity measures, which are the subject material for this chapter, are based on data collected by the value stream manager and summarized using manual or electronic spreadsheets. The box score is the primary measurement tool used for communicating and managing capacity.

The capacity section is configured as the middle section of the box score for a reason: it provides the link between operational and financial performance. As operational improvements are achieved through lean initiatives, the capacity measures will generally improve—moving nonproductive capacity to available capacity. The value stream team will then be able to proactively plan to use the freed capacity for growth. This chapter explains how to measure productive, nonproductive, and available capacities.

Capacity Measures

In order to manage capacity, you need to identify what your productive, nonproductive, and available capacities are for each value stream. To help you understand how to determine these capacity measures, we will use an example that looks at the capacity of production employees in an order fulfillment value stream. Similar calculations can be done to assess the capacity of machines and facility space.

The data in Table 6.1 depict a partially completed capacity portion of a monthly box score for an order fulfillment value stream. We have referred to this as the Mass value stream. The box score capacity section has three categories of capacity: productive, nonproductive, and available. Besides the current and prior monthly capacity figures, a target future state for December 31 (fiscal year end) is shown on the capacity section of the box score. Your company will likely want

Table 6.1 Mass Value Stream Box Score—Capacity Section for the Month Ending September 30

	Capacity	Aug 31	Sept 30	Oct 31	Nov 30	Target Dec 31
Employee	Productive	62.6%	**65.6%**			70.0%
	Nonproductive	33.4%	**35.2%**			15.0%
	Available	4.0%	**−00.8%**			15.0%
Machines	Productive	33.4%	33.4%			45.8%
	Nonproductive	42.7%	40.7%			26.2%
	Available	23.9%	25.9%			28.0%

to initially target capacity improvements of one capacity type. The capacity type chosen will depend on the mix of labor and machine usage in your production process and the resource that presents the biggest constraint to flow and pull. As you progress further on your lean journey, you may want to begin to analyze additional types of capacity.

Box Score Capacity Measures

The capacity measures reported at the value stream level are derived from monthly calculations completed at the cell level, which are then transferred to the capacity section of the value stream box score. If appropriate for your company, these calculations could be reported weekly rather than monthly. The bottleneck cell determines the flow through the value stream, so the capacity measures of the bottleneck cell are the capacity measures reported on the value steam report. The other cell capacity measures are primarily relevant for helping to improve the bottleneck cell capacity. Of course, the bottleneck cell may change as you make improvements to the current bottleneck's capacity.

The example we present will demonstrate, step by step, how to calculate the highlighted employee capacity numbers shown in Table 6.1 for the month of September. A complete list of the steps is found in Table 6.2. The data shown in Table 6.3 represent the September capacity information collected by the Mass value stream managers and cell team leaders. These data are used in simple calculations to arrive at the summary capacity measures depicted in Table 6.4. The value stream managers will then use this information to discuss capacity issues as well as other box score items.

The following example provides some direction to assist you in developing a dataset for determining your capacity measures. Although the example measures employee capacity, the same process is used when calculating machine capacity. Capacity measures can quickly become complex, but as much as possible, we want to avoid any unnecessary complexity, since lean promotes simplicity and relevance.

Table 6.2   Steps for Measuring and Managing the Capacity Section of the Box Score

Step 1	Collect monthly data by work cell.
Step 2	Calculate productive, nonproductive, and available capacity for each cell.
Step 3	Determine the bottleneck cell.
Step 4	Transfer capacity measures of the bottleneck cell to the box score.
Step 5	Review with management and target improvement possibilities.
Step 6	Tie lean improvements to changes in capacity and improved operation measures.
Step 7	Use freed-up capacity to improve financial performance.

Table 6.3   Mass Value Stream Cell Data Collected for the Month of September (Step 1)

Data Labels	Cell-Level Measures	Time Frame	Cell 1	Cell 2	Cell 3
A1	Total units processed (include rework)	Month	92,000	86,000	84,000
B1	Average employee cycle time per unit	Seconds	11	8	10
C1	Scrap rate per units processed	N/A	10%	10%	10%
D1	Rework rate per units processed	N/A	20%	16%	18%
E1	Average batch size	N/A	500	500	500
F1	Average setup time per batch	Minutes	15	8	10
G1	Average inspection percentage per units processed	N/A	10%	10%	10%
H1	Average inspection time	Seconds	10	10	10
I1	Number of shifts	Day	2	2	2
J1	Crew size	Shift	8	6	8
K1	Working hours	Shift	7.5	7.5	7.5
L1	Working days	Month	20	20	20
M1	Idle time per month	Minutes	2,400	1,400	720
N1	Meeting times per employee per month	Minutes	120	120	120
O1	5S time per employee per month	Minutes	100	100	100

Note: In this example, each person with a machine cell performs a task on each product that flows through the cell. In cell 1, for example, eight people spend an average of 11 seconds with each unit, totaling 88 seconds per unit. All information represents average production for a month.

Table 6.4A   Mass Value Stream Capacity Calculations for Productive Capacity

Description	Formula and Calculation for Cell 1	Capacity in Minutes
Total Available Time		
Total available time (A2) = number of shifts per day × crew size per shift × working hours per shift × working days per month × 60 (converts hours to minutes)	A2 = I1*J1*K1*L1*60 A2 = 2 × 8 × 7.5 × 20 × 60	144,000
Productive Capacity Time		
Productive capacity time (B2) = total units processed × average employee cycle time × crew size per shift × first time through (1.00 – [scrap rate + rework rate])/60 seconds	B2 = A1*B1*J1*(1 – [C1 + D1])/60 B2 = (92,000 × 11 × 8 × 0.7)/60	94,453
Productive Capacity Percent (transferred to box score in Table 6.1)		
Productive capacity % (C2) = productive capacity time/total available time	C2 = B2/A2 C2 = 94,453 ÷ 144,000	65.6%

Step 1: Collect Monthly Data by Cell for the Capacity Spreadsheet

You want measures that are easy to collect, report, and understand, yet give you a good approximation of available capacity and capacity improvements. Table 6.3 lists typical data that are needed to calculate cell employee capacity. The data components will likely vary if you are measuring another type of capacity. The data labels, e.g., A1 and B1, are used for reference in the Table 6.4 calculations.

Step 2: Calculate Productive, Nonproductive, and Available Capacity

Data collected in step 1 and shown in Table 6.3 are used in calculating various capacity components. These calculations are shown in detail in Table 6.4 and are used to determine the total available time and the percentage of productive capacity (6.4A), nonproductive capacity (6.4B), and available capacity (6.4C). The summary measures shown in Tables 6.4A,B,C are inserted into Table 6.5. For simplicity, we use minutes as the measure of time. You may find that seconds are a more appropriate unit of measure for your process.

Step 3: Determine the Bottleneck Cell

In our example, cell 1 of the value stream has 65.6% productive capacity, 35.2% nonproductive capacity, and –00.8% available capacity. Most value streams and

Table 6.4B Mass Value Stream Capacity Calculations for Nonproductive Capacity

Data Labels	Description	Formula and Calculation for Cell 1	Capacity in Minutes
Nonproductive Capacity Percent (transferred to box score in Table 6.1)			
D2	Rework and scrap time = (total units processed × average employee cycle time × (scrap + rework rate) × crew size per shift)/60 seconds	D2 = (A1*B1(C1 + D1)*J1)/60 D2 = (92,000*11*(0.10 + 0.20)*8)/60	40,480
E2	Setup time = total units processed ÷ average batch size × average setup time per batch	E2 = A1/E1*F1 E2 = 92,000 ÷ 500 × 15	2,760
F2	Inspection time = total units processed × average inspection percentage × average inspection time	F2 = (A1*G1*H1)/60 F2 = (92,000 × 0.10 × 10)/60	1,533
G2	Meetings = meeting times per employee × number of shifts × crew size per shift	G2 = N1*I1*J1 G2 = 120 × 2 × 8	1,920
H2	5S work = 5S time per employee × number of shifts × crew size per shift	H2 = O1*I1*J1 H2 = 100 × 2 × 8	1,600
I2	Total nonproductive time = the sum of the minutes attributable to rework and scrap, downtime, setup time, inspection time, meetings, and 5S work	I2 = D2 + M1 + E2 + F2 + G2 + H2 I2 = 40,480 + 2,400 + 2,760 + 1,533 +1,920 + 1,600	50,693
J2	Nonproductive capacity % = nonproductive time ÷ total available time	J2 = I2/A2 J2 = 50,693 ÷ 144,000	35.2%

Table 6.4C Mass Value Stream Capacity Calculations for Available Capacity

Data Labels	Description	Formula and Calculation for Cell 1	Capacity in Minutes
Available Capacity Percent (transferred to Box Score in Table 6.1)			
K2	Available capacity time = total available time − (productive time + nonproductive time)	K2 = A2 − (B2 + I2) K2 = 144,000 − (94,453 + 50,693)	−1,146
L2	Available capacity % = 100% − [productive capacity % + nonproductive capacity %]	L2 = 1 − (C2 + J2) B2 = 1 − (0.656 + 0.352)	−00.8%

Table 6.5 Mass Value Stream Employee Cell Capacity Measures for the Month of September

Data Labels	Employee Capacity (all time units are in minutes)	Cell 1	Cell 2	Cell 3
A2	Available time	144,000	108,000	144,000
B2	Productive capacity time	94,453	50,912	80,640
C2	**Productive capacity %**	**65.6%**	**47.1%**	**56.0%**
Nonproductive Time				
D2	Rework and scrap	40,480	17,888	31,360
M1	Idle time	2,400	1,400	720
E2	Setup time	2,760	1,376	1,680
F2	Inspection time	1,533	1,433	1,400
G2	Value stream meetings	1,920	1,440	1,920
H2	5S work	1,600	1,200	1,600
I2	Total nonproductive time	50,693	24,737	38,680
J2	**Nonproductive capacity %**	**35.2%**	**22.9%**	**26.9%**
K2	Available capacity time	–1,146	32,351	24,680
L2	**Available capacity %**	**–00.8%**	**30.0%**	**17.1%**

cells will have a positive number for available capacity. In fact, it is generally considered desirable to have at least 10% available capacity in order to have some flexibility. Cell 1 actually shows a slight negative for available labor capacity. This means that they currently have to pay overtime in order to process the 92,000 average monthly units in cell 1. Table 6.5 shows that cell 1 is the bottleneck cell since it is the cell with the lowest available capacity.

Step 4: Transfer Capacity Measures of the Bottleneck Cell to the Box Score

Only the bottleneck (cell 1) capacity measures in the highlighted boxes (productive capacity %, nonproductive capacity %, and available capacity %) of Table 6.5 are transferred to the capacity section of the weekly box score found in Table 6.1. As indicated earlier, this is because the bottleneck cell basically determines productivity; in a pull environment, it constrains the flow in all of the cells.

Step 5: Review with Management and Target Kaizen Possibilities

The cell-level details as presented in Table 6.5 provide information that guides the focus of kaizen events that address bottleneck issues restricting capacity. For example, it is easy to see that process quality improvements are greatly needed within cell 1's operations, since the rework rate is 20% and the scrap rate is 10%. In other words, only 70% of the 92,000 units processed result in good product. Until the bottleneck issues in cell 1 are resolved, the company must resort to using costly overtime labor to meet production demand whenever the monthly quantity produced is approximately 92,000 units or above. This limits the company's ability to grow. Alternatively, the company could consider efforts to rebalance the cells to shift available labor capacity from cell 2 to cell 1. This could be easy or difficult depending on the skills needed to perform the work in cell 1 compared to cell 2.

As stated earlier, most firms would like to have a minimum of 10% available capacity in order to have some flexibility. Our example firm decided on two strategies to help free up cell 1 capacity. First, it focused on making process improvements in cell 1 by scheduling a kaizen event to create a *poka-yoke* that would cut the rework rate in half—from 20% to 10%. This allowed cell 1 to rebalance the workload and cut the cycle time from 11 seconds to 9 seconds. Balancing the workload increases flow throughout the value stream, decreasing the overall lead time to produce one finished unit.

The second capacity-increasing effort was to cross-train employees. The value stream manager recognized that some of the excess labor capacity in cell 2 could be used in cell 1. With some cross-training and slight modifications of work distribution, a cell 2 worker was able to work half time in cell 1 and half time in cell 2. Cross-training workers gives value streams more flexibility in meeting customer demand.

Step 6: Tie Lean Improvements to Changes in Capacity and Operational Measures

Table 6.6 presents the results from our strategies to free up capacity and eliminate overtime work in cell 1 through workload balancing and cross-training. As shown, available capacity increased substantially in cell 1, with negligible impact to cell 2. Because cell 1 had been a significant bottleneck constraint before the lean improvements, the additional capacity available in cells 2 and 3 had gone unused.

With these lean improvements, the overall capacity of the Mass value stream has gone from −00.8% to 16.5%, making room for the company to in-source some components or sell more units without additional conversion costs. The immediate effect was that the number of good units produced increased by 9,200 because fewer units in cell 1 required rework. The newly freed-up capacity in the bottleneck cell provides opportunities for the value stream to increase profits from the sales of 9,200 more "cost-free" units. Not only do capacity and financial measures improve, but operational measures—such as throughput time and rework rate—also improve. As mentioned earlier, the middle section of the box score—capacity—has ties to both the operations section and the financial section of the box score.

Table 6.6 Mass Value Stream Capacity Measures after Kaizen Improvements

Data Labels	Employee Capacity	Cell 1	Cell 2	Cell 3
A2	Available time	153,000	99,000	144,000
B2	Productive capacity time	93,840	46,669	80,640
C2	**Productive capacity %**	**61.3%**	**47.1%**	**56.0%**
Nonproductive Time				
D2	Rework and scrap	23,460	16,397	31,360
M1	Idle time	2,400	1,400	720
E2	Setup time	2,760	1,376	1,680
F2	Inspection time	1,533	1,433	1,400
G2	Value stream meetings	2,040	1,320	1,920
H2	5S work	1,700	1,100	1,600
I2	Total nonproductive time	33,893	23,027	38,680
J2	**Nonproductive capacity %**	**22.2%**	**23.3%**	**26.9%**
K2	Available capacity time	25,267	29,304	24,680
L2	**Available capacity %**	**16.5%**	**29.6%**	**17.1%**

Note: Improvements include process changes reducing rework, cross-training, and improving cycle time. Other than the rework rate, cycle time, and crew size, the other capacity data elements remain the same as those shown in Table 6.5 for the month of September.

The capacity analysis can be further extended to classify costs into the following three categories: value-added (from a customer's perspective), non-value-added (costs that represent wasted resources), and non-value-added but necessary (necessary for the functioning of the organization but non-value-added from the customer's perspective). Returning to our labor capacity analysis of cell workers, Table 6.7 presents an example of cell worker capacity data that is similar in nature to the data shown in Table 6.6. We can summarize the hours spent in each of the three categories. Time spent producing good product is value-added time (220,000 hours). Hours recorded under of the headings of scrap, rework, and idle time would be non-value-added (80,000 hours). Hours recorded for inspection, value stream meetings, 5S work, and unused available capacity (100,000 hours) would be non-value-added from a customer's perspective, but are necessary to the orderly operation of our business and the principles of lean management. Some excess capacity—a minimum of 10% is often recommended—should be allowed to accommodate fluctuating demand and unforeseen stoppages.

Table 6.7 Example of Value-Added versus Non-Value-Added Cost Analysis

	Hours	*%*	*Payroll*
Cell Workers (all cells)			
Value-added time	220,000	55.0	$4,400,000
Non-value-added (NVA)	80,000	20.0	160,0000
Non-value-added, necessary	40,000	10.0	80,0000
Available time, NVA necessary	60,000	15.0	120,0000
Total cell workers	400,000	100.0	$8,000,000
Maintenance Workers			
Value-added time	0	0	0
Non-value-added	2,500	20.0	$50,000
Non-value-added, necessary	10,000	80.0	200,000
Total maintenance workers	12,500	100.0	$250,000
Value Stream Management and Staff			
Value-added time	0	0	0
Non-value-added	45,000	.30	$225,000
Non-value-added, necessary	105,000	.70	525,000
Total VS management and staff	150,000	100.0	$750,000
Value Stream Total			
Value-added time	n/a	48.9	$4,400,000
Non-value-added	n/a	40.3	3,625,000
Non-value-added, necessary	n/a	10.8	975,000
Value stream total		100.0	$9,000,000

This analysis is just one small part of the necessary analysis of value-added versus non-value-added costs. It represents personnel costs in an order-fulfillment value stream. Table 6.7 adds the costs of non-cell workers to arrive at total personnel costs broken down into the three categories. This same thinking and analysis should be applied throughout all value streams and support functions and should include all cost categories (not just personnel costs). This is the strategic information that can help upper management answer this question: For every dollar of cost incurred, what percent is value-added? Answering this question, relating it to our overall strategic objectives, and trending the data will provide insight not provided by traditional financial statements. This analysis of value-added versus non-value-added costs should be a supplemental schedule that provides addition key information about the cost categories on value stream financial statements.

Without a clear picture of the before value stream capacity and the after value stream capacity, the company would not have a full understanding of the bottleneck issues, such as what is creating the bottleneck, what it can do to improve the capacity through the bottleneck, and what the results are from improvements in the bottleneck cell. Of course, it is always important to remember that conditions are never static, and once we solve one bottleneck issue, a new constraint will arise and need our attention. The "journey" always continues!

Step 7: Use Freed-Up Capacity to Improve Financial Performance

Lean is a growth strategy. One of the central benefits of lean is realized when nonproductive capacity becomes available capacity. Nonproductive capacity essentially is capacity being used in non-value-added activities. Thus, turning nonproductive capacity into available capacity generally occurs with minimal additional investment in people or equipment. The revenue per dollar of conversion costs will grow exponentially when new sales opportunities fill freed-up capacity. Companies must determine whether their strategic approach is to grow the market share of their current products or introduce new products with strong margins and high customer value. If neither of these options is a viable firm strategy, then in the long term, unused capacity can be reassigned, discarded, or sold to further reduce overall value stream conversion costs.

Space Management

Space is a critical resource for many companies. Buying, building, or leasing space is a very expensive investment. As illustrated in Chapter 4 on value stream costing, it is important to highlight how much space is actually being used by a value stream team, in order to better understand how much space is available for other activities. As value stream teams implement improvements that reduce the amount of space they actually use, the benefit is immediately evident in the value stream cost statements, as the cost associated with the unused space appears in the sustaining cost column as unused space. That amount triggers discussion by management on how to productively use that space.

The capacity calculations described in this chapter focus on a single value stream. As managers step back and look at the overall facility with multiple value streams, a composite capacity measure is useful. Referring back to Chapter 4, Figure 4.3 presents a value stream cost statement for a plant consisting of two order fulfillment value streams and one new product development value stream. Sustaining costs summarizes both office space and unused plant capacity. A facility-level box score would report capacity percentages reflecting the actual usage of the entire facility, as shown in Table 6.8.

Table 6.8   Facility Capacity Summary

Facility Capacity	May 2013	June 2013	Target
Order fulfillment value streams	85.5%		88.0%
New products value stream	3.8%		4.0%
Office	3.2%		3.2%
Available	7.5%		4.8%

Summary

Capacity management is an important lean concept that is often overlooked in traditional companies. Tracking the productive and available capacity for our value streams contributes to our understanding of how we are progressing on our lean journey. As we make improvements, we free up capacity, which affects decisions about outsourcing, taking on new projects, and growing our business. In this chapter, you were introduced to the essential steps for managing capacity and simultaneously improving value stream performance. As you learned how to calculate percentages for productive, nonproductive, and available employee capacity, it became evident that tracking and calculating capacity can quickly become complex. As with all lean concepts, it is important to keep these calculations as simple and relevant as possible. Capacity measures are generally reported on the box score. Normally the capacity and operational measures on the box score will show improvement before the financial effects of lean are reflected. The box score is an excellent visual tool for showing the results from kaizen improvement initiatives to free up capacity over time. This important feedback allows value stream managers and upper management to see the progression of their lean journey and make better decisions regarding future business.

Discussion Questions

1. Why is capacity management important in a lean environment? What decision making in your company would be improved with a better understanding of your capacity usage?
2. What is the most important step in capacity management? Explain why you think it is critical.
3. Why would available capacity ever be negative?
4. What is a reasonable target to have for a cell's available capacity percentage? What are some of the improvement initiatives that you could take at your company to free up available capacity?
5. If cell 3 in the example were to improve its rework percentage by 25%, reduce its batch size by 50%, and reduce its inspection of units processed to 8%, how would the available capacity percentage be affected?
6. What are some of the most critical activities that affect your company's nonproductive capacity percentage?

Chapter 7

Product Costs and Lean Decisions

In earlier chapters, we learned that unit standard costs do not fairly represent the cost of a product. This unit cost, however, is typically used as a baseline to compare alternatives for many decisions, such as pricing, special orders, make-or-buy decisions, and product mix decisions. Once you implement lean accounting, standard costs should no longer be used or maintained, and new decision tools that are more aligned with lean principles must facilitate comparing alternatives. Fear Box 7.1 poses the biggest question in a manager's mind: "How do I make decisions without unit costs?"

At the end this chapter, you should be able to do the following:

- Understand why using unit product standard costs are generally ineffectual for decision making in a lean environment.
- Use features and characteristics costing to guide pricing decisions.
- Determine the optimal product mix using throughput margins.
- Assess special orders and make vs. buy scenarios to maximize the value stream.

Throughput and Conversion Costs

There is one key concept that is the foundation for product-related decisions in a lean environment—the impact of throughput on conversion costs. Throughput is the number of units that can be produced throughout a production cell in a given time. The determining factor is the bottleneck process. No matter how long it takes the other workstations to process the part, a cell cannot produce more than the bottleneck constraint. Figure 7.1 depicts four different products that are produced in the same work cell with five workstations. Each product requires different processing at each workstation. Adding the time from all workstations, product A takes

**FEAR BOX 7.1: HOW DO I MAKE DECISIONS
WITHOUT A UNIT PRODUCT COST?**

This is a fair question. Managers have been using traditional reporting methods to make a variety of product-related decisions. Regardless of these methods' accuracy, they are comfortable with the format, and they have appeared successful using these "tried and true" tools. As traditional tools—such as standard costing—are recognized as obsolete and ineffective, managers must learn how to use new tools for these decisions that are guided by lean thinking.

18 minutes to produce. Product B takes the same amount of total time, but only utilizes four of the five workstations. Products C and D both utilize all five machines, but the processing time increases to 23 minutes and 25 minutes, respectively.

Standard Costing Method

Using the standard costing method, labor cost for one unit would be calculated using the total labor time, while overhead cost would consider the machine time at each workstation. Table 7.1 breaks down the costs for each product using the standard costing method. Two methods for overhead allocation are illustrated. The first is the simplest and most commonly found in practice. It uses labor hours as the basis for allocation. The second separates the time by machine and applies a separate overhead rate for each machine. This is often the case when there is a variety of machine sizes that consumes varying levels of resources. You can see that the two methods track very closely. As the total processing time increases for each product, the total cost increases as well.

Throughput Method

For the throughput method, the first step is to identify the bottleneck process for each product. This is the workstation that takes the longest amount of time to process one unit. For products A and B, the bottleneck is workstation C, which processes one unit every 6 minutes. The most that can be produced in 1 hour is 10 units (60 minutes/6 minutes per unit). The processing time of the other four workstations does not really matter as long as each one of the workstations processes in less than 6 minutes. For example, workstation D for product A takes 2 minutes to process. Even if that time is doubled to 4 minutes, it would not slow down the production cell. The cell would still be capable of producing

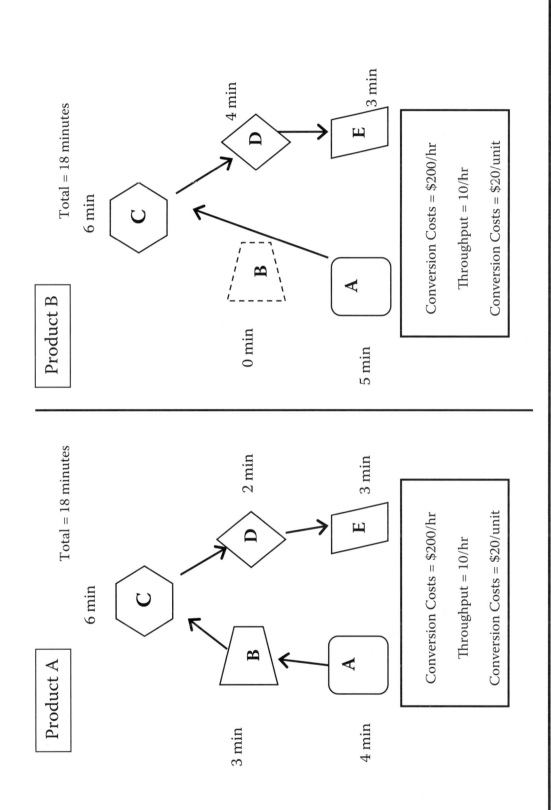

Figure 7.1 Throughput and conversion costs.

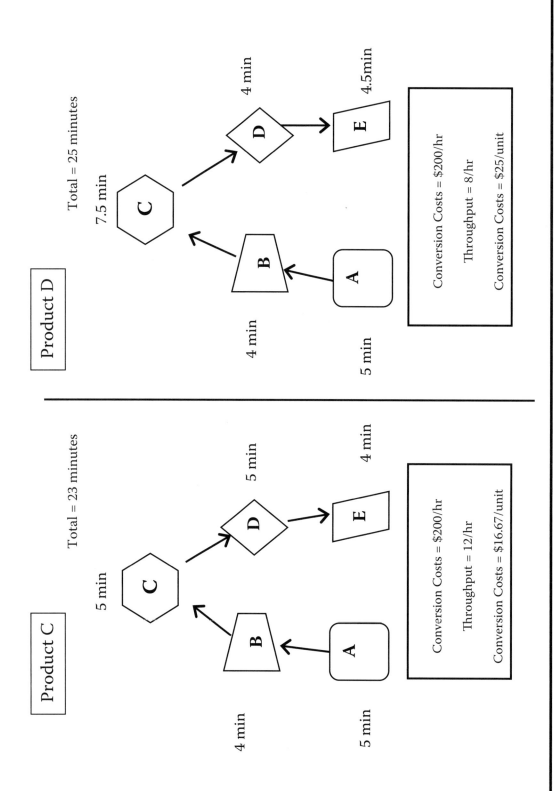

Figure 7.1 (continued) Throughput and conversion costs.

Table 7.1 Comparison of Costing Methods

	Product A	Product B	Product C	Product D
Method 1				
Material	$9.00	$9.00	$9.00	$9.00
Labor	$3.60	$3.60	$4.60	$5.00
Overhead	$8.40	$8.40	$10.73	$11.67
Total	**$21.00**	**$21.00**	**$24.35**	**$25.67**
Method 2				
Material	$9.00	$9.00	$9.00	$9.00
Labor	$3.60	$3.60	$4.60	$5.00
Overhead	$8.38	$8.02	$10.62	$11.62
Total	**$20.98**	**$20.62**	**$24.22**	**$25.62**
Method 3				
Material	$9.00	$9.00	$9.00	$9.00
Conversion cost	$20.00	$20.00	$16.67	$25.00
Total	**$29.00**	**$29.00**	**$25.67**	**$34.00**

Calculations: Method 2: Overhead Cost by Machine Time

		Product A		Product B		Product C		Product D	
Workstation	Machine OH Rates per Hour	Minutes per Machine	OH Cost	Minutes per Machine	OH Cost	Minutes per Machine	OH Cost	Minutes per Machine	OH Cost
A	$28.00	4	$1.87	5	$2.33	5	$2.33	5	$2.33
B	$32.00	3	$1.60	0	$0.00	4	$2.13	4	$2.13
C	$26.00	6	$2.60	6	$2.60	5	$2.17	7.5	$3.25
D	$23.00	2	$0.77	4	$1.53	5	$1.92	4	$1.53
E	$31.00	3	$1.55	3	$1.55	4	$2.07	5	$2.58
Total		**18**	**$8.38**	**18**	**$8.02**	**23**	**$10.62**	**25.5**	**$11.82**

Note: Costing methods:

Method 1: Standard costing with overhead allocated based on labor hours.
Method 2: Standard costing with overhead allocated based on machine time.
Method 3: Throughput method with the optimal number of throughput units.

Assumptions:

1. The material used in each product is identical and costs $9 per unit.
2. Direct labor rate is $12 per labor hour.
3. For method 1, overhead is allocated on the basis of labor time using an average overall rate of $28 per hour.
4. For method 2, overhead rates vary by machine center and are applied using the time on specific machines.

10 units every hour. Nor would reducing the time at workstation D by half—to 1 minute—affect how many units can be made in an hour. That is because the time at the bottleneck machine has not changed. The bottleneck of a process is often referred to as the constraint because it restricts the volume that can flow through the cell.

So what happens when the time at the constraint changes? Look at product C where the time at the constraint is reduced to 5 minutes. This means that throughput increases and 12 units can be made in 1 hour (60 minutes/5 minutes). The opposite occurs for product D. Here the time at the constraint increases to 7.5 minutes. This reduces the number of products that can be made to eight per hour (60 minutes/7.5 minutes). The second step of the throughput method is to consider the throughput units for applying conversion costs. Conversion costs are the costs of all the resources (e.g., labor and machines) required to transform raw material into a finished product for the customer. In our example, the conversion costs equate to $200 per hour. The conversion cost per unit is calculated by dividing the conversion cost per hour by the throughput units for each product. For example, products A and B both produce 10 units an hour. Therefore, the conversion cost for one unit is $20 ($200 per hour/10 units per hour). To this we add material and component costs to obtain an estimated unit product cost. Table 7.1 provides the details behind the product cost calculations.

Figure 7.2 compares unit costs using both the two standard costing methods (labor or machine hour allocations) and the throughput method. Two striking differences immediately become visible. First, the standard costing method is consistently estimating product cost considerably lower than the throughput method. Since the conversion costs for the throughput method are applied for each workstation per the time on the bottleneck, the unused capacity is incorporated into the product costs, unlike the standard costing method, which only accounts for the actual minutes of production in its labor and overhead costs. Second, unit cost for product C decreased using the throughput method, while it increased using standard costing! This is because there is no relationship between total processing time and the number of units that can be produced in a given time

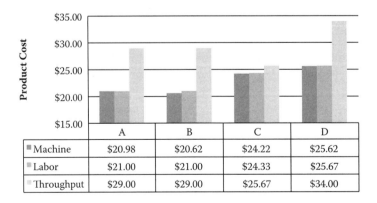

	A	B	C	D
■ Machine	$20.98	$20.62	$24.22	$25.62
■ Labor	$21.00	$21.00	$24.33	$25.67
■ Throughput	$29.00	$29.00	$25.67	$34.00

Figure 7.2   Comparison of standard costing (machine and labor allocations) and throughput methods.

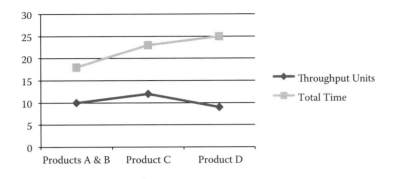

Figure 7.3   Comparison of total processing time and throughput units.

(see Figure 7.3). The total processing time for product C has increased, causing the unit cost to increase under the standard costing system. However, under the throughput method, product C unit costs decrease due to the decrease in the constraint time and the corresponding increase in throughput.

Product Pricing Decisions

When it comes to setting a product's price, the customer is really the final arbiter. Sales and marketing, however, need to have a good idea of what a product costs in order to inform sales negotiations. Features and characteristics costing is used for this purpose. It is based on the premise that a product's cost is determined by the features that consume different resources from other products. Two factors need to be considered: material and conversion costs.

Material and components, such as lumber or hinges, are specific to an individual product. Different versions of the same product may require different materials. These differences are reflected in the cost. As we have just seen, conversion costs per unit are a function of how long it takes to process on the bottleneck. Table 7.2 presents an example of how features and characteristics costing works. The company in this example makes a product that consists of two materials— one steel block and several gaskets. The bottleneck in the production cell is the drilling machine. This machine can drill two holes at one time in a steel block, although it can be adjusted to drill only one hole if necessary. A gasket is needed for each hole drilled.

Table 7.2   Example: Features and Characteristics Costing

No. Holes Drilled	2	3	4	5	6	7	8
Material: Steel block	$10.00	$10.00	$10.00	$10.00	$10.00	$14.00	$14.00
Material: Gaskets ($0.50 each)	$1.00	$1.50	$2.00	$2.50	$3.00	$3.50	$4.00
Conversion cost	$5.50	$6.00	$6.00	$6.50	$6.50	$7.00	$7.00
Estimated product cost	$16.50	$17.50	$18.00	$19.00	$19.50	$24.50	$25.00

←———— Anchor ————→

The cost of the steel block and number of gaskets are directly assigned to each drilling configuration. The most common configuration of this product requires four holes and gaskets and is highlighted in the table. Conversion costs are calculated using the same process described earlier. As you can see, the conversion cost increases with each insertion of the drill bit because that is the feature that determines the time on the bottleneck. The more time required on the constraint, the more conversion costs the product consumes. The less time required, the fewer conversion costs consumed. The result of this analysis will be a matrix that can be used by salespersons to help with sales negotiations.

Product Mix Decisions

In a situation with limited capacity and demand for multiple products, the question is, "Which product will yield the most profit?" Traditional methods compare unit costs in different scenarios and decisions favor the product with the highest gross margin per unit. Lean methods recognize that the labor and other resources at the cell remain materially the same. The difference comes back once again to throughput.

Table 7.3 contains information used in subsequent analyses, including the cost of product components, sales dollars and units, and the number of units that can be produced at each workstation in 1 hour. Using this information, Table 7.4 compares two methods: standard costing and lean accounting. The standard

Table 7.3 Operating Information for LMEC

	Plastics Value Stream		
	OS1	TX4	KC13
Unit cost (standard costing model)			
Material	$0.093	$0.148	$0.129
Labor	$0.046	$0.069	$0.050
OH	$0.086	$0.148	$0.148
Total unit cost	$0.225	$0.365	$0.327
Sales dollars	$195,118	$399,642	$432,003
Units sold	542,960	684,319	825,694
Units processed per hour:			
Injection	2,040	1,650	2,050
Heat treating	2,320	n/a	2,200
Cutting and splicing	2,560	2,110	n/a
Assembly and pack	2,760	2,600	2,400

Table 7.4 Product Mix Decisions

	OS1	TX4	KC13
Standard Costing Model			
Unit sales price	$0.359	$0.584	$0.523
Standard unit cost	$0.225	$0.365	$0.327
Gross margin	$0.134	$0.219	$0.196
Lean Accounting Model			
Unit sales price	$0.359	$0.584	$0.523
Material cost	$0.093	$0.148	$0.129
Throughput margin	$0.266	$0.436	$0.394
Throughput units per hour (injection)	2,040	1,650	2,050
Throughput dollars per hour	$543	$719	$808

costing model analysis favors producing the TX4 because the margin per unit is higher than that for the other products.

The lean accounting model considers the impact of throughput units in the framework. First, material cost is subtracted from sales price to calculate a throughput margin per unit. This is multiplied by the number of units that can be made on the bottleneck machine for that product in 1 hour. The result is throughput dollars per hour, and more closely represents the amount of dollars that are available to pay for conversion costs and profit. In contrast to the standard costing method, KC13 is the product that generates the most dollars per hour. The key reason for the different results is that the traditional method does not consider throughput units. The lean accounting model compares the dollars generated in 1 hour by each product.

Special Order Decisions

It is common for a company to receive an offer to buy a large quantity of product at a reduced price. Sometimes the order requires special processing as well. The traditional method for assessing whether to accept the order is to use a per unit analysis that captures incremental revenue and costs to determine whether the return is acceptable.

Lean thinking seeks to maximize the profit for the value stream as a whole, rather than by individual product. The question becomes, "Is the value stream more profitable if we accept this order?" To answer this question, compare the current value stream cost statement to what it would look like if the order is accepted.

Table 7.5 Special Order Decisions

Incremental Unit Product Cost Model		
	Standard Product	*Special Order*
Sales price	$52	$46
Material costs	$15	$16
Direct labor	8	9
Total overhead	10	11
Unit cost	$33	$36
Margin	$19	$10
Return on sales (ROS)	36.5%	21.7%

Value Stream Cost Model (in thousands)		
	Current State	*Future State*
Revenue	$1,730	$1,776
Material costs	$655	$671
Conversion costs	785	785
Total value stream costs	$1,440	$1,456
Value stream profit	$290	$320
Return on sales (ROS)	16.8%	18.0%

Let us look at an example to illustrate both methods. Assume that LMEC has capacity to accept a special order received for 1,000 units of the product at $46 per unit. The customer order requires stitching an extra patch costing $1 each onto the product. Table 7.5 compares the special order with our standard order. LMEC typically sells this product for $6 more than the offer and earns 36.5% return. The special order includes increased material and labor costs to apply the patch, and the return on the order is reduced to 21.7%. Comparing the two margins and returns, it would be very difficult to accept the order because acceptance would reduce the overall profitability of the product.

In the value stream cost model, however, we see a different story. Accepting the special order actually increases the value stream return by 1.2%. This analysis favors accepting the order because it increases the profit of the value stream as a whole. What are the key differences between the analyses? First, the value stream cost statement captures all products and product families in the value stream rather than one specific product. This explains why the value stream return on sales (ROS) is lower than the single product. Second, the incremental cost model treats direct labor as a purely variable cost tied to the product, while the value stream cost model treats labor as fixed and part of the conversion cost.

One concern often raised in special order decisions is price erosion. How low can the price fall before it impacts the greater market? Excellent question! Most of these decisions are made at the operations level and not always with access to the greater market view. To ensure pricing strategies remain intact, some companies employ a pricing specialist who has a 20,000-foot view of the market and can have final word on questionable orders.

Make vs. Buy Decisions

A make vs. buy decision may also be called outsourcing. The make/buy analyses for both the standard costing methods and the value stream model follow the same premises as the special order decision. In traditional thinking, the make unit cost is compared to the buy unit cost, and a decision is made based on the lower of the two unit costs. In the value stream model, the focus is on which option will increase the value stream profit as a whole.

Table 7.6 presents both types of analyses for a product. LMEC is currently manufacturing 1,000 units and is considering whether or not it would be better

Table 7.6 Make vs. Buy Decisions

Incremental Unit Product Cost Model		
	Make	*Buy*
Material costs	$8	$0
Direct labor	10	0
Variable overhead	6	0
Purchase cost	0	20
Unit cost	$24	$20

Value Stream Cost Model (in thousands)		
	Current State (Make)	*Future State (Buy)*
Revenue	$1,730	$1,730
Material costs	$655	$647
Purchased goods		20
Conversion costs	785	785
Total value stream costs	$1,440	$1,452
Value stream profit	$290	$278
Return on sales (ROS)	16.8%	16.1%

to buy the product from a vendor. The total internal cost for making this product has been determined to be $24 per unit, and it can be purchased externally for $20. This includes the cost of drop shipping directly to the customer's warehouse. Incremental unit cost under this analysis shows that it would cost $4 more to make the product.

The value stream analysis compares the current state that includes making the product to what the value stream would earn if the product were purchased. In this example, the ROS is actually higher if LMEC continues to manufacture the product internally. Again, the fundamental difference in determining whether or not to outsource is related to available capacity. If capacity is available, the incremental conversion costs to make the product are minimal or effectively free. Thus, any costs (e.g., labor, overhead, shipping) above your additional material costs that you pay to an outsourcer are unnecessary premiums.

What if this decision has more complex issues? For example, LMEC may need to consider the opportunity costs of other alternative production possibilities. These opportunity costs can (and should) be included in future state analyses. Providing several different "what if" scenarios helps to make the decision factors more apparent.

Note: Certainly these decisions are not just tied to financial numbers. LMEC must also consider nonfinancial factors such as customer service, shipping time, quality control, technology expertise, impact on new product development, employee availability, and supplier reliability.

Box Score Format

In Chapter 3, the box score format was introduced as a way of keeping both key operational and financial metrics in front of decision makers. It can also be a very useful decision-making tool for comparing alternatives. In fact, it makes good sense to do so. If the measures on the box score are the key performance indicators (KPIs) we want monitored, then we should evaluate the effects from different scenarios on our KPIs. Table 7.7 shows how useful the box score format can be for a decision with two alternatives.

Summary

The four types of decisions we discussed in this chapter are common situations that confront managers on a regular basis. Traditional accounting methods have provided frameworks to help with these decisions—but are typically not aligned with the objectives of lean thinking.

Table 7.7 Using a Box Score to Compare Alternatives

	Current State	Future State Alternative 1	Future State Alternative 2	Planned Future State 12/31/xx
Operational Metrics				
On-time shipment	98.0%	94.0%	93.2%	98.0%
Dock-to-dock days	23.58	20.50	20.50	16.50
First time through	46%	42%	43%	50%
Average product cost per unit	$388.16	$348.66	$352.77	$316.91
Capacity				
Productive	10.8%	10.8%	11.5%	24.7%
Nonproductive	54.8%	54.8%	52.6%	23.4%
Available	34.4%	34.4%	35.9%	51.9%
Financial Metrics				
Revenue	$1,101,144	$1,280,400	$1,265,000	$1,408,440
Material cost	$462,480	$512,160	$530,240	$535,207
Conversion	$250,435	$231,884	$240,444	$208,696
Return on sales (ROS)	22.5%	23.2%	21.2%	26.3%

The key is to remember the fundamentals. In a lean environment, we want to optimize the performance of the entire value stream, rather than individual products. An important contributing factor is how we choose to utilize our capacity. One objective of lean is to free up capacity by eliminating waste. It is very critical to have a growth plan in place to utilize that capacity as quickly as possible. Finding new markets and new products, and in-sourcing previously outsourced product are good ways to use that capacity and optimize the value stream. These lean decision frameworks provide input to help make choices that support lean organizational goals.

Challenge

Will these lean decision frameworks work in your company? Here is a challenge: identify a sampling of special order or make vs. buy decisions made in the last two months at your firm. Apply the new framework. Would you make the same recommendation using the lean decision approach? Some may be the same, but you will most likely find that using the lean decision frameworks will yield better (and more intuitive) decisions!

Discussion Questions

1. Explain why unit product costs are not essential in a lean manufacturing environment.
2. What is the main determinant for decision making related to optimal product mix for cells and value streams? How can a standard costing system provide faulty information on product mix?
3. Compare the throughput method to a standard costing system. Why would the unit product costs differ between the two methods?
4. How do lean manufacturers most appropriately determine whether or not to accept special orders or to outsource? What is the key determinant?
5. Discuss features and characteristics costing. When is it necessary to use it?
6. How can the box score format support decisions such as whether or not to make or buy a part?

Chapter 8

Lean Planning

In this chapter, we will discuss the different facets of planning in a lean organization. We will see that planning happens at several organizational levels and over time frames of different lengths, and that planning and control are intricately linked. Lean planning is an integrated process that is based on the learning that occurs throughout the plan, do, check, act (PDCA) cycle. The different levels of planning are linked through a mechanism that attunes long-term strategy to daily organizational activities. At all levels of planning, the ultimate purpose is to deliver to the customer the right product at the right time with the least amount of waste. In order to do this, a lean organization must be able to both anticipate future customer demand for products and services and establish the capacity to meet this customer demand. A lean organization also allows for flexibility in demand and continually monitors available capacity and the rate of demand or pull from the customer.

Lean planning takes a somewhat different point of view than traditional planning. There are four planning levels: (1) long-term strategic planning, (2) mid-term hoshin kanri (which is often referred to as policy deployment or strategy deployment), (3) short-term sales, operations, and financial planning (SOFP), and (4) weekly or daily production planning. Each planning level has a different time horizon and level of detail. All planning initiatives should work together to achieve organizational objectives. Proper planning activities flow from the top strategies of the organization down to the production floor, where level scheduling is designed to meet customer demand. As you will see, all four levels of planning are linked together and can be viewed in light of the PDCA model.

Lean planning and traditional financial budgeting should be treated as complementary processes during the initial stages of lean accounting implementation. As your company matures in its adoption of lean accounting methods and lean management systems, traditional financial budgeting will likely be recognized as unnecessary, counterproductive, and wasteful. But typically, an organization needs several years of establishing control within its processes before it is ready to give up the perceived financial controls provided by budgets. As we will discuss, the use of linked planning processes (long, medium, and short term) and real-time performance feedback metrics actually provide better control than the monthly comparison of micro-detailed financial results to annually prepared micro-detailed budgets.

By the end of this chapter you should be familiar with the following:

■ Lean planning and the PDCA cycle.
■ The difference between traditional planning and lean planning.
■ The levels of planning in a lean organization: strategic planning, hoshin kanri (strategy deployment), SOFP (sales, operations, financial planning), and operations scheduling.
■ The linkages among strategic planning, hoshin planning, SOFP, and operations scheduling.

Lean Planning and the PDCA Cycle

What is lean planning? It is the processes needed to develop the future strategies, goals, and action plans envisioned by a lean organization. Lean planning includes the appropriate methods for providing the right combination of inputs (e.g., material, labor, machines, outside processes, and facilities) at the right time to produce products or services that meet customer demand. Lean planning is carried out at different levels and time horizons—from broad, long-term strategic planning to daily, short-term operations scheduling. Long-term, mid-term, and short-term plans are linked through cascading A3's (or layered X-matrices) that become more detailed as time frames shorten and planned actions become more closely associated with the one-piece-flow production cycle. All planning should be considered in reference to the PDCA (plan, do, check, act/adjust) cycle.

The PDCA cycle was originally conceived by Walter Shewhart in the 1930s and later adopted by W. Edwards Deming. The dynamic PDCA cycle presents a scientific method for gathering data, hypothesizing about future conditions and market demand, and developing action plans to make improvements and meet company needs given the environment and market demand. The four phases of the continuously flowing PDCA cycle are discussed below (see Figure 8.1).

Plan. In the planning phase, opportunities for change and improvement that offer the most return for the effort are analyzed. The planning stage begins with the gathering of data, such as production problems, capacity usage, value stream profitability, and takt time. The data are used to form hypotheses about future conditions and market demand. Information about what opportunities exist for change or improvement often will come

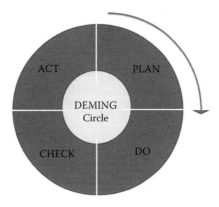

Figure 8.1   Deming circle.

from the performance metrics gathered through lean accounting methods. Planning includes developing the specific steps that are needed to achieve improvement goals.

Do. The do phase is the operational part of the PDCA cycle where you implement the improvements designed in the plan stage. This do phase can be thought of as the day-to-day management of the business in moving toward the future planned state.

Check. This is also sometimes referred to as study (PDSA). Checking involves gathering data on key value stream performance measures that monitor the success or failure of countermeasures, taking into consideration the environment and market demand. In this critical stage, you should ask the following questions: Are we improving and making progress toward our intended future state? What have we learned? What went right? What went wrong? It is important to determine how well your countermeasures support achievement of the intended future state results.

Act. In the act (or adjust) phase of the PDCA cycle, you will review the data and determine whether to continue with the strategy outlined in the plan phase of the cycle or whether it is prudent to respond with a different action plan. If changing conditions or unforeseen roadblocks have hampered success from your original plan, appropriate adjustments will need to be made, which leads you back to the initial planning stages. Supportive of the lean philosophy, the PDCA cycle is a never-ending cycle of continuous improvement.

Integrating the PDCA concepts within the planning process of the company generates continuous performance evaluations at all levels of the company. The current state is analyzed using data gathered through performance metrics, hypotheses for achieving an improved future state are postulated and tested, action plans are developed through the involvement of everyone on the team, and performance metrics are designed to gather information about how well the action plans are working to achieve the desired future state. The box score, introduced in Chapter 3, serves several important functions in the PDCA cycle. Organizations plan across various time horizons—the upcoming week, the next quarter, the next year, and future states that are several years out. Thus, the box score can be used to track past, current, and projected operational, capacity, and financial measures for the various levels of planning. It can also be used for sensitivity analysis in comparing different projected future scenarios, as discussed in Chapter 7.

Lean Planning vs. Traditional Planning

Traditional Planning—The Annual Budget

There are several major differences between traditional planning and lean planning. We will begin with a brief discussion of a traditional organization where planning is associated primarily with the budgeting process. The annual budgeting process for the operating profit and loss (P&L) budget begins with a sales forecast, which leads to a production schedule and standard cost setting for labor, material, and overhead (used to calculate cost of sales and to value inventory). Expense budgets are also prepared for the nonproduction departments. Preparing cash and capital spending budgets is another part of the annual budgeting process. When all budget schedules are completed, they are then rolled up to a master budget for the organization.

Budgets are often prepared by initially looking back at the prior year's expenses and determining how the next year's expenses are expected to fluctuate based on future expected sales demand and other factors. Budgeting is an extremely time-consuming, game-playing annual mental exercise that may span several months, only to be quickly outdated as circumstances change, which they invariably do. Yet, the budget continues to be used as a control tool as well as a planning tool; actual results are compared to budgeted sales and expenses to determine variances between the two. Managers are held responsible for unfavorable variances—which helps to explain the all too familiar human behavioral factors associated with "gaming" in traditional budgeting. Managers understandably work to safeguard themselves from the negative consequences of underperforming the budget.

Most annual budgets are prepared as static budgets, which are nonresponsive to current market conditions. Since they are not dynamic, they are unable to reflect the changing demand of customers, and often force companies to miss out on unexpected opportunities. Another downfall of budgets is that they are too focused on financial outcomes and are typically expressed as forecasted, pro forma financial statements, even though no one—not even top management—can predict the future. Further, budgets provide limited insight into operational requirements, operational inputs, and capacity. The overall result of the traditional budgeting process is that it is generally an effort in futility—a non-value-added, unproductive, tremendously time-consuming activity that wastes valuable company resources.

FEAR BOX 8.1: HOW CAN WE CONTROL COSTS IF WE DON'T HAVE A BUDGET?

 One of the biggest fears many companies experience as they move further down the path of lean accounting is how to control the business if they don't have detailed budgets. But the question that must be asked is: How much control is provided by a budget that was developed in the last half of the prior year, with the information available at the time, and that is nonresponsive to "real-time" conditions? Performance reports are prepared each month that compare budget to actual, and report a wide variety of variances to management. These performance reports provide little insight into the day-to-day processes of the business that produce value or generate waste. In fact, performance reports may even promote counterproductive behaviors such as overproducing or buying material in large quantities. Problems are difficult to identify and correct because the transactions affecting the results have occurred anywhere from one week to five weeks prior. In contrast, lean planning provides control through real-time visual management of processes, weekly reporting of results, standardized work, and empowerment of people.

Lean Planning—A Different Focus and Process

The lean planning process, on the other hand, is designed to meet the management needs of the company and, because of its dynamic nature, overcomes many of the shortcomings of traditional budgeting. The purpose of lean planning is to develop action plans to attain the strategic goals of the company.

The motivation behind lean planning is multidimensional—focusing on operational inputs (material, labor, machines) needed to meet customer demand, capacity needs and availability, and financial outcomes. It is a flexible planning process that adjusts operational levels as customer demand fluctuates—continually assessing capacity availability and reacting to customer pull.

Lean planning uses either an A3 or an X-matrix to communicate (1) the intended future state, (2) the actions needed to attain the future state given the current state conditions, (3) the measurements (both financial and nonfinancial) that will be used to track how well the plans are accomplishing the intended goals, and (4) responsibility assignment for specific actions. (For excellent discussions on the specifics of using the A3 format, refer to *Getting the Right Things Done* by Pascal Dennis (2007) and *Managing to Learn* by John Shook (2010). Refer to *Hoshin Kanri for the Lean Enterprise* by Thomas L. Jackson (2006) for an explanation of the X-matrix.)

Lean planning is done at the value stream level and then rolled up to a facility or enterprise level. Responsibility for developing ongoing plans and the resulting assessment features embedded in lean management remains at the value stream level. Critical feedback is attained from such assessments as value stream and cell performance metrics, standardized work procedures, kanban systems, 5S audits, value stream maps identifying improvement needs, and action reports.

Because lean budgets are generally updated every quarter on a rolling 12-month horizon, they are prepared much more efficiently. There is no long, grueling process required to game through the annual budget. In traditional planning, cost centers are identified at the departmental level, creating a silo effect. This can cause unforeseen problems. For example, a cost reduction in one department may lead to a cost increase in another department. Purchasing could reduce the number of orders and freight charges by ordering large lot sizes, but this would likely increase warehousing, obsolescence, and moving costs. Efforts to maximize individual departmental performance seldom lead to maximization of organizational performance. In lean companies, costs are viewed at the value stream level. Efforts are made to minimize total costs across the value stream without sacrificing quality, customer value, or total cycle time. In fact, a cost increase in one area may ultimately improve the overall operation of the company if it increases flow, quality, or customer value. This can be more easily identified when planning is done at the value stream level, rather than at the department level.

Traditional plans often fail to consider capacity issues, whereas operational capacity is a major focus of lean planning. Effective analysis of the company's capacity on both machines and employees to meet planned demand should uncover bottlenecks that will disrupt flow, as well as excess capacity that can be used for growth opportunities or special orders. Lean planning also includes the selection and use of performance metrics at the enterprise, value stream, and cell levels. Lean management practices require frequent review of the daily and weekly metrics, particularly at the cell and value stream levels. For example, value stream metrics should provide weekly information on average cost, dock-to-dock time, number of defects, etc. Cell performance is monitored daily (and often by the hour) to quickly uncover quality

LEAN IN ACTION 8.1: RECOGNIZING AVAILABLE CAPACITY

Under its old decision model that was based on traditional costing, LMEC turned down "good business" for which it had (but did not recognize) the capacity to accept. LMEC managers now use their monthly SOFP meetings to analyze capacity and update their operating plans. Identifying unused capacity allows them to better evaluate the consequence of accepting special orders, which generally do not add any (or only minimal) additional conversion costs. Including capacity analysis as part of a frequent planning update has led to an increase in profitability for the company.

Table 8.1 Traditional Budgeting vs. Lean Planning

	Traditional Budgeting	*Lean Planning*
Focus	Financial outcomes	Multidimensional: operational inputs, capacity, financial outcomes
Format	Pro forma financial statements, expressed primarily in dollars	Cascading A3's or X-matrix that contain financial and nonfinancial data
Time frame	One year	Capacity horizon
Planning cycle	Annual static planning process	Ongoing, updated quarterly
Time to complete	Months	Days
Cost centers	Departmental silos	Value streams
Ties to operational capacity	No	Yes
Control mechanism	Analyze variances from budget	Report and act upon performance data collected at the value stream and cell levels
Motivation	Budget "padding" in anticipation of higher-level "cuts"	Team unity toward achieving strategic objectives

(defect rates) and delivery (making to takt time) problems. The standard work of management also includes oversight of the continuous improvement process. As problems are found, they are documented and an action plan is designed to address them. Follow-up by the value stream manager ensures that appropriate countermeasures are found and implemented.

This system of selecting performance metrics, taking frequent measurements, and responding immediately to problems provides a level of control that is not possible through the traditional practice of analyzing monthly variances from the budget. Lean planning motivates team unity toward achieving improvements, in contrast to the arbitrary, game-playing tactics of traditional budgeting.

Table 8.1 summarizes the major differences between traditional budgeting and lean planning in the areas of focus, format, time frame, planning cycle, time to complete, cost centers, ties to operational capacity, control mechanisms, and behavior motivation.

Four Levels of Lean Planning

There are four levels of lean planning: strategic planning, hoshin planning, SOFP, and daily or weekly production planning. The following paragraphs describe each of the planning levels. It is important to remember that all levels of planning are linked together in such a way that the strategic plans cascade down to the hoshin plans, which cascade down to SOFP, which cascades down to production plans for the day or week. The performance metrics associated with the action plans developed at each planning level should also have linkage that ties them all together. (Refer to Chapter 19 in *Practical Lean Accounting* by Maskell et al. (2012) for a discussion and diagram of performance linkage charts.)

Level 1: Strategic Planning

In order to develop a meaningful strategic plan, it is critical to understand your customer and your capabilities, as well as the vision of your company. Lean planning begins at the strategic level where decisions about the company's vision and long-term business strategies are developed. A macro-level PDCA cycle sets overall parameters for lower levels of planning. At this level, upper management looks out over a time period that normally ranges from 3 to 5 years. Broad-ranged decisions about market segments, products, marketing strategies, customer groups, and capital financing policies are developed to provide direction for the company that is in alignment with its vision. This is sometimes referred to as the "true north" of an organization, and is at the top of a cascading set of action plans.

Similar to the traditional budgeting process, traditional strategic planning can be bereft with problems. In his book *The Rise and Fall of Strategic Planning*, Mintzberg (1994) describes the many problems of strategic planning, including (1) arbitrary goals that are not linked to the firm's capabilities, (2) too many goals lacking focus, (3) planned activities that are not regularly reviewed, (4) planning as an event rather than a process, (5) inadequate organizational communication leading to disconnects both horizontally (within departments) and vertically (between departments), (6) inadequate use of data in the planning process and overanalysis of subsequent data, and (7) a punitive review process that leads to gaming. Strategic lean planning, on the other hand, is the starting point of an integrated process that has continuous improvement at its foundation. The long-term vision and goals of the company are identified, and true north is established.

Level 2: Hoshin Planning (Strategy Deployment)—Medium Term

The next level of lean planning is referred to as hoshin planning (also called hoshin policy deployment or hoshin strategy deployment). Hoshin planning is typically done on an annual cycle, but should be updated on a quarterly basis or as needed. Hoshin plans are used to determine required production cycle times, to create level schedules, and to plan the people and equipment that will be needed. The plan generated by the hoshin process is hierarchical in nature. Top management's vision, strategic goals, and broad parameters for the upcoming planning cycle are translated into cascading levels of action plans starting from the enterprise level, down to the value stream level, and finally to the cell level. This results in the alignment of strategies and action plans throughout the entire organization, with each level of management supporting the goals of the level that is a step higher up in the hierarchy. Every strategy is assigned tactics or actions that need to be undertaken to accomplish the strategy.

The Japanese words *hoshin kanri* can be translated into "direction setting." Hoshin planning encourages the involvement of all employees in the direction-setting process. Optimal results can only be achieved if everybody in the organization fully understands the goals of the company, the planned actions, and the metrics used to measure progress toward the desired future state. To be truly effective, the hoshin planning process must incorporate cross-functionality and promote intra- and interprocess cooperation. The view of the company must be across the value streams, which is in contrast to traditional budgeting that is done within departments. *Catchball* is a term that refers to the process by which team leaders elaborate and communicate the hoshin plan to all teams in the organization. It is also known as *nemawashi*, which is the back-and-forth exchange of ideas between management and employees. Using catchball, there is a lot of back-and-forth exchange among the parties in negotiating the team charters that govern the experiments of the hoshin process.

Hoshin planning is a step-by-step planning process that uses the PDCA cycle—a systems approach to the management of change in a company's business processes and operations. It is an involved, intricate process that will take your company time to learn. Because of the complexity and importance of hoshin planning, we recommend that you have a sensei help you through the process of establishing hoshin planning in your company. When used correctly, it will accomplish the meaning of the Japanese term *hoshin kanri*—it will point your company in the "right direction." We refer the reader to two books for better understanding of hoshin kanri: *Getting the Right Things Done* by P. Dennis, and *Hoshin Kanri for the Lean Enterprise* by T. L. Jackson.

Level 3: Sales, Operations, and Financial Planning (SOFP)—Short Term

Traditionally managed companies will typically hold monthly review meetings to assess the prior month's results and any variances from the annual budget. In lean companies, the critical component of successfully implementing your company's strategy is through the SOFP process. This lean planning standardized process is conducted every month within each value stream. The final and culminating step of the SOFP process is the executive planning meeting, where all the value stream plans are rolled up into an overall plan for the organization that should be linked to its strategic goals. Critical to the success of SOFP is the achievement of three important conditions: (1) support by top management so that SOFP becomes a formally organized process that is part of the culture of the organization, (2) responsibility for the planning process and execution of the plan must be by the same people, and (3) recognition of the SOFP process as an integral part of value stream management.

The SOFP process originates at the value stream level and requires a team approach for several reasons: (1) information comes from several sources; (2) planning must be integrated among new product development, sales and marketing, production operations, materials management, financial management, and support personnel; and (3) the action plan must be understood, agreed upon, and supported by all of the value stream members.

Various outlets contribute inputs to the SOFP process. Sales and marketing (which in some companies is a separate value stream) provides forecasts of expected sales for the next 12 months, while product development (also a separate value stream in some companies) provides data about new product introductions and changes to existing products. Production (usually referred to as the order fulfillment value stream) provides information about the available employee and machine capacity of the value stream, and finance (a support function) provides detailed financial and accounting information at the value stream level.

The outcome of the SOFP process is an integrated plan for each value stream that is tied not only to the overall objectives of the value stream but also to the overall objectives of the company. It becomes the "game plan" that guides sales personnel, product development personnel, operations, and support personnel. An effective SOFP process gets everyone working together toward accomplishing the same objectives.

Steps in the SOFP Process

The steps included in the monthly SOFP process are outlined below. Steps 1 through 4 and step 7 are performed at the value stream level. Steps 5 and 6 are performed at the enterprise (or facility) level. Information for the SOFP planning process is gathered by the value streams, with support from functional experts in the controller's office.

> **Step 1—Forecast sales.** Product and account managers forecast sales demand based upon input from customers, the sales force, history, and market trends. The forecast is reviewed for accuracy. The outcome of the demand planning is a new set of monthly sales forecasts for the upcoming planning horizon (anywhere from 9 to 18 months, with 15 months being a typical time period) for each product family within each of the value streams.
>
> **Step 2—Identify resource requirements.** Based on information developed in step 1, the resources required to satisfy the production needs for the sales forecast are broken down and assessed for each month (a box score is useful for depicting this information), taking into account the newly forecasted product mix and the bottlenecks (or constraints) within the value stream flow.

Step 3—Assess capacity needs. Required capacity to satisfy the sales forecast demand is compared to available capacity, which is based upon current resources and previously planned acquisitions of additional resources. It is important at this point to consider the anticipated capacity gains that will result from kaizen events and other continuous improvement efforts.

Step 4—Review combined value stream requirements. The value stream planning teams come together in a joint meeting to review at a plant (or enterprise) level the SOFP information they have generated. The goal of this step in the process is to optimize the capacity usage and profitability of the combined value streams. This meeting provides an opportunity for the value stream teams to evaluate ways to assist each other and to propose solutions for problems both within and across value streams. An outcome of this meeting is an agenda for the SOFP executive planning meeting that contains a detailed action plan for review and approval.

Step 5—Project support and capital needs. The controller's office performs the roll-up and analysis of value stream and general support projections, including capital forecasting and balance sheet projections. The financial outcome of these plans are calculated and depicted as monthly "planned" measures for the financial section of the box score.

Step 6—Review with executive team. The executive planning meeting is held, which is led by the CEO and includes the executive team and value stream managers. It is important that adequate preparation and carefully prepared reports at the value stream level result in an effective, focused meeting at the executive level. The primary tasks of this meeting are (1) reviewing the operational and financial data prepared by the value streams, (2) attending to any decisions that must be made at the executive level, and (3) and approving the action plan and its execution.

Step 7—Follow through with action plans. The final step of the SOFP process is attending to the details needed to meet the plan's objectives. At the operations level, it includes creating level schedules for the upcoming months of the planning period, establishing the value stream takt times and cycle times, and staffing the cells so a balanced workload is accomplished. Identified changes in capacity needs, determined in the planning process, are also addressed. Where shortages of capacity were recognized, action is taken to acquire additional resources. If available capacity was identified, opportunities to use (or reduce) the capacity are explored.

Value streams operating with a successfully executed SOFP process become "well-planned, well-coordinated, and flexible lean organizations" (Maskell et al., 2012, p. 236). *Practical Lean Accounting* by Maskell et al. (2012) presents a more detailed description of the SOFP process.

LEAN IN ACTION 8.2: LMEC'S MONTHLY SOFP PROCESS

Days 1–2: Value stream demand planning. Product/account managers forecast sales demand based upon input from customers, sales force, history, and market trend. The forecast is reviewed for accuracy. (Steps 1 and 2.)

Days 3–5: Value stream operations planning. Value stream teams evaluate labor and machine capacity, material availability, and capital needs, based on the sales forecast. (Steps 3 and 4.)

Days 6–7: Financial planning. The controller's office performs the roll-up and analysis of value stream and general support projections, including capital forecasting and balance sheet projections. (Step 5.)

Day 8: Executive SOFP meeting. Top executives perform a brief review of the past month's results, review each value stream's projections and issues, review the topside financial roll-up, and make decisions regarding the path forward to position the company to meet sales demand and company profit targets. (Step 6.)

The SOFP Schedule

The SOFP process begins after the monthly close and the gathering of essential information. Lean in Action 8.2 depicts the SOFP schedule for LMEC, which can be generalized to most companies. Please note that day 1 of the process does not represent the first day of the month, but rather the first day of the SOFP process, which would correlate to your company's closing process and when the required information is available.

Level 4: Weekly Planning Meetings

The last level of planning occurs on a weekly basis and consists of a value stream "stand-up" meeting where the production operations for the upcoming week are scheduled. The weekly stand-up meeting is also part of the value stream's feedback mechanism. The prior week's cell and value stream-level performance metrics are reviewed and problem areas are identified and discussed. This is an opportunity for the value stream manager to involve the entire value stream team in planning continuous improvement efforts. It is also one of the major mechanisms to ensure control within the lean enterprise. Visual management, timely identification and resolution of problems, and involvement of the entire value stream team are all hallmarks of a lean enterprise system.

Summary of Lean Planning

In this chapter we have discussed the planning process of a lean organization. Lean planning is proactive and avoids many of the common pitfalls of traditional planning. It is an integrated process that is based on the learning that occurs throughout the PDCA cycle. Lean planning is multidimensional, including operational inputs, capacity analysis, and financial impact. It is primarily performed at the value stream level. It brings about team unity toward achieving organization goals and continuous improvement.

We have seen that planning happens at four levels: strategic planning, hoshin planning, SOFP, and weekly value stream meetings. All levels of planning are linked together in a cascading set of hierarchical A3's or X-matrices.

Discussion Questions

1. What are the main differences between lean planning and traditional budgeting?
2. When organizations understand the gaming of most traditional budgeting systems, why are they so reluctant to change the process?
3. Discuss which phase of the PDCA cycle you think is most critical and why.
4. Explain what is meant by a lean budget.
5. Why is understanding capacity critical for lean firms?
6. How do you determine how often to track and update performance metrics?
7. Discuss how companies can effectively align their strategies throughout their organization.
8. What is the best approach to effectively implement hoshin planning?
9. What must organizations do to make their weekly planning meetings valuable?
10. Who are the most important players in the SOFP process? What are their responsibilities?

References

Dennis, P. 2007. *Getting the right things done*. Lean Enterprise Institute, Cambridge, MA.
Jackson, T. L. 2006. *Hoshin kanri for the lean enterprise*. Productivity Press, New York.
Maskell, B., B. Baggaley, and L. Grasso. 2012. *Practical lean accounting*. 2nd ed. CRC Press, Boca Raton, FL.
Mintzberg, H. 1994. *The rise and fall of strategic planning*. Free Press, New York.
Shook, J. 2010. *Managing to learn*. Lean Enterprise Institute, Cambridge, MA.

Chapter 9

Measurement Selection and Alignment

There are three reasons why there is a tendency to measure what we have measured in the past. First, we want to maintain meaningful comparisons with history. The premise is that even if we know a measure isn't perfect, at least we can see if it changed, and maybe that change will highlight something we should know. The reality is that if a measure is not already meaningful, then a historical trend won't make it more meaningful. The second reason is that we have always measured it this way, and we trust that the person who established the measure did so for a good reason. The truth is that processes change over time, and what may have been a reasonable indicator in the past may no longer fit the bill. Finally, we are reluctant to change measurements because there is a cost to change. It takes time and effort to determine the best measurements, establish tracking mechanisms, and implement change. Users of the information need to understand the reasons for the change and how to interpret and use the improved information.

It is important that we start with the fundamentals of why we measure. One reason is to support decision making by providing feedback, identifying problems, and measuring progress toward goals. Measures provide a periodic status of processes and trigger corrective actions. Another reason for measurement is to evaluate outcomes and strategy. It is necessary to take a step back and assess outcomes, assign accountability, and reward performance. This allows management to see when a change of course is needed in order to meet strategic objectives.

Lean organizations *must* reevaluate their performance measurements in light of the new way they do business. This chapter addresses the reasons why measures must change, explains how to identify appropriate measures, and outlines how to align measures with strategy in a lean organization. By the end of this chapter, you should be able to do the following:

- Understand why measures must change.
- Describe the distinction between input, process, and output measures.
- Fully comprehend why lean needs appropriate process measures.
- Select and align meaningful goals and measures.
- Understand why measuring knowledge work is challenging.
- Methodically select knowledge work measures that minimize risk.

Reasons for Change

The goal of management accounting information is to provide the necessary data and information for decision making. There are three key reasons why management accounting information must change in a lean environment.

1. **The goals of the system have changed.** The goal of a traditional system is to facilitate increased efficiency and lower cost per unit. Consequently, manufacturing in larger batches is encouraged because this means fewer changeovers and larger price breaks on materials, leading to lower costs. However, batch processing does not consider the hidden costs of inventory movement, storage, obsolescence, and damage. Even service and support areas process batches of reports, invoices, etc. The real cost, however, is the lack of flexibility and increased working capital that processing in large batches requires.

   The primary focus of a lean system is not on reducing the cost per unit, but in creating and managing balanced, quality, and efficient processes. The goal is to produce and deliver 100% quality products and services, in a smooth flow, and on time. By focusing on constantly improving processes and shortening lead times, flexibility and capacity increase without large capital investments. Working capital requirements decrease as order-to-invoice time reduces. The overall effect is improved cost efficiency.

2. **The organizational structure has changed.** Traditionally managed organizations are vertically structured with department managers responsible for decision making and budget accountability. Accounting reports comparing actual spending with predesigned budgets are targeted toward these managers. Lean organizations are flatter and more horizontal. Cross-functional value stream teams are now responsible for most operational decisions. It makes sense that accounting information should target value stream teams rather than functional departments and managers that are no longer relevant.

3. **The timing of information needs has changed.** Accounting is a transactional control system designed to provide summaries of activities to managers so that they can assess whether or not their areas are "in control." In other words, variance reporting in the form of departmental expense reports and profit and loss reports indicate whether individual areas met

expectations as defined by the annual budget. Traditional reporting reliant on accounting cycles is done monthly. By this time, the magnitude of any problem is usually larger because it was not caught and communicated right away.

In a lean system, value stream teams need to know in real time when a process is "out of control." Visual management is a critical element of any lean system because it alerts all users immediately of the status and needs of the process in time to make corrections before more problems occur.

For these three reasons—changes in system objectives, organizational structure, and timing of information—it is critical to examine the relevancy of the accounting information currently provided in our organizations.

Measurement Selection

It is not easy to select the measures that provide the best information to decision makers. This is illustrated below with an example to which many of us can relate:

> Tom has been trying to get into shape by working out regularly and making better food choices. He gauges how well he is doing by monitoring his weight on the bathroom scale every Monday morning. When the scale doesn't show enough progress, Tom immediately cuts way back on his food intake to see if that makes a difference. If that doesn't work, he becomes frustrated and starts working out harder. Judging his performance with scale weight is an "end of process" measure. The problem with this is that it doesn't point to modifications Tom should make to drive him toward his objectives. It doesn't answer the right questions, such as: Should Tom change his food choices? Is he eating enough protein? Should he cut back on carbs? How should his activity level change? Does he need more cardio workouts? Should he increase the weights during his strength training? Answering these questions requires tracking his *process* rather than just the *outcome*.

Just as Tom is using a measure to monitor his progress in order to achieve his goal, managers also use measures to monitor progress. The question is whether managers are choosing the best measures for their purpose. Figure 9.1 depicts how products and services are provided. Material is transformed into a product or service valued by the customer through conversion processes requiring skilled people, and resources, such as equipment and innovations. Output measures are good for historical tracking, planning strategy, and monitoring overall progress toward strategic goals. They are key when determining if a change of course is necessary. Measurement systems, however, that focus only on output measures don't highlight where changes are needed. The result is a series of trial-and-error troubleshooting with reliance placed on instinct and prior experiences. This can be costly in both time and investment, and the actual cause of the problem may

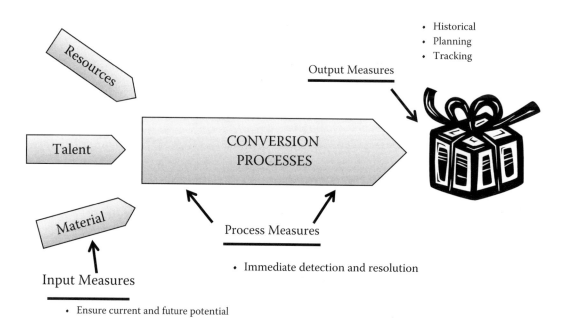

Figure 9.1 Input–Process–Output model.

still prove elusive. Problem solving needs to be data driven to address the root cause of problems so that solutions prevent future occurrences.

The purpose of process measures is to immediately detect problems or issues so that they can be resolved as quickly as possible *and* before more of the same problems occur. This is the primary focus of lean systems—highlighting and resolving problems when they happen. Monitoring the critical points of the process is essential to produce a quality product or service delivered to the customer on time. Input measures are often overlooked but are important to ensure current and future potential. Material quality, worker capability assessment, and innovation development help to meet current needs as well as to grow capabilities.

Measures are used to guide decisions—it follows that determining what and how to measure must start with the decision to be made. Is it tactical, such as the number of products to ship that day? Or is it more strategic, such as whether to expand a product line? Generally, for more tactical decisions, measures are needed more frequently and closer to the work. If the measures are more strategic, they are more relevant to those higher in the organization and are viewed less frequently. Identifying how the information will be used and by whom leads to a better understanding of what information is needed for decision making.

Once the appropriate information for the required decision is thoroughly understood, the next phase is to focus on the measures themselves—how they are calculated and where the data reside. This is where the "devil is in the details" takes over. It is important to explicitly walk through the measurement collection and calculation process. Determine what data are currently available and where they are found (e.g., which computer system, area). If data are not already available, how will they be collected and who will be responsible for

Table 9.1   Key Measurement Questions

Decide	1.1 What is the decision being made?
	1.2 Who is involved in the decision?
	1.3 What information is needed to inform the decision?
	1.4 Who is responsible for the result?
Measure	2.1 How is the measurement calculated?
	2.2 Where are the data located?
	2.3 Who is responsible for collecting and reporting the measure?
	2.4 At what level is the measure pertinent (e.g., cell, initiative, facility)?
	2.5 How frequently should it be reported (e.g., hourly, daily, weekly)?
Review	3.1 Is the measure for immediate use, such as daily shipping reports? Or should the measure be reviewed at weekly staff meetings?
	3.2 How will the measure be communicated (e.g., metric board, shift meetings, monthly report)? What is the level of visibility required to take notice?
	3.3 How do we track countermeasures and follow-up actions?

beginning collection? Can collection be automated or does it need to be done manually? How frequently should the measures be collected and reported? Who is accountable for reporting the information and who is responsible for the results?

Measures need to be reviewed at intervals appropriate for their purpose. Table 9.1 contains measurement questions that will help to guide you through reviewing the key points about your metrics. Metric boards for cells on a manufacturing floor are updated daily, and some even hourly. Metric boards for value streams are more infrequent, but are usually reported weekly. Monthly measurement reviews are most appropriate at the factory or business unit level. Along with frequency, consideration must be given as to how the measures are communicated. Visual management is a key component of lean practices. Visual boards in meeting rooms, break rooms, and on manufacturing floors are common. Visual management and communications are discussed in more detail in Chapter 10. Table 9.1 outlines questions to facilitate measurement development.

Measures and Alignment

It isn't enough to thoughtfully and explicitly consider what we are measuring and how the decision is used. We must also ensure that managing with those measures will lead us toward meeting the company's goals. It is essential, therefore, for the management team to engage in a process that aligns measures and goals throughout the levels of the organization. This section describes the process LMEC used to ensure measures were aligned throughout the organization.

Table 9.2 Examples of Work Cell and Value Stream Measures

Examples of Work Cell Measures	
Quality	• Number of defects • Rework
Smooth flow	• Operational equipment effectiveness • Day-by-the-hour (DBH) metric • Takt time
Delivery	• Percent orders shipped complete and on time • Percent lines shipped on time • Percent orders shipped < 5 days late, < 10 days late, etc. • Percent of accurate orders shipped
Safety	• Hours down due to safety mishap • Number of reportable events • Lost work days • Safety audit results
Competencies	• Skills tracking • Vacation scheduling • 5S charts
Examples of Value Stream Measures	
Inventory management	• Inventory by type • Days supply of inventory • Inventory change and direction
Throughput	• Order-to-invoice time • Dock-to-dock days • Sales dollars per value stream employee • Value stream cost per units shipped
Customer service	• Percent orders shipped complete and on time • Percent lines shipped on time • Issues and actions tracking
Value stream profit	• Value stream profit before inventory changes • Inventory changes • Average product cost
Competencies	• Skills tracking • Vacation scheduling • 5S charts

Process

LMEC used a mapping process to align measures and goals from top management right down to manufacturing cells. For LMEC, this meant aligning through three levels: company, value stream, and work cells. There are four key benefits to using this process. First, mapping measures to goals ensures that all goals do indeed have measures to monitor progress. Second, talking through possible measures and selecting the most appropriate ones highlight redundant measures that may already exist. Third, the mapping process itself encourages discussion about processes and how the goals and measures overlap. Fourth, the end result is a set of measures that the value stream supports because they helped to develop them. Consequently, the value stream team members are more likely to manage their operations using these measures.

Level 1: Company Strategies and Goals

The first step of the alignment mapping process is company strategy. Figure 9.2 provides an alignment example of our sample company, LMEC. The goals of LMEC are (1) to be the best employer and (2) to be the best in the industry. To achieve these goals, LMEC's top leaders established five strategic objectives: profitable growth, premier customer service, safe and secure work environment, optimal resource utilization, and effective processes. The leadership team also developed measures that would gauge the operation's progress toward these goals. The leadership team needs to monitor progress so that they can determine if a change in strategic course is necessary. Appropriate measures, therefore, are collected at an overall facility level. It may be that one measure supports more than one goal. For example, return on net assets (RONA) provides information related to two goals—resource utilization and effective processes.

Level 2: Value Stream Goals and Measures

Once leadership has defined the strategic objectives and measures, it is the value stream team's turn to develop the balance of the goals and measures. The purpose of the value stream team is to manage the entire end-to-end process. Its chief concerns are continuous improvement, smooth flow, removing obstacles, and ensuring quality and customer service. The team is mindful of these as they develop goals and measures. For each strategic measure, the core value stream team asks, "What must the value stream do really well to influence this strategic measure?" Once the team agrees upon the value stream goals, the next step is to determine how to measure progress toward each goal For example, how will we know if the flow through the value stream is improved? Figure 9.3 shows three measures to gauge improved flow. *Value stream cost per unit* (total value stream cost/number of units shipped) will monitor how well product is "pulling"

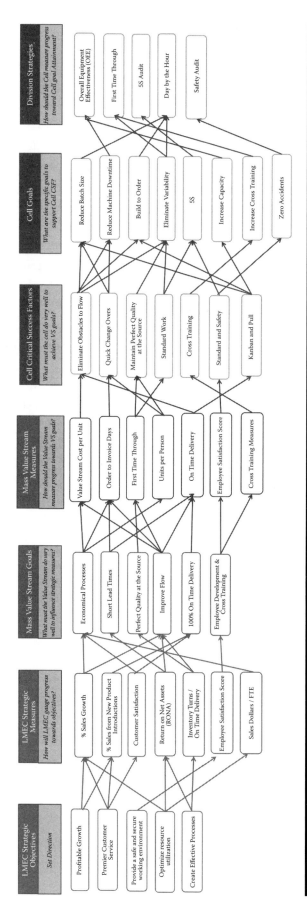

Figure 9.2   Alignment diagram from the Mass Value Stream at LMEC.

through the processes by customer orders. Inventory built without orders will appear as spikes. *Order-to-invoice* days will benchmark and monitor improvement by showing the average number of days it takes for a customer order to be processed, shipped, and invoiced. Order-to-invoice days will reduce as flow improves. The third measure is *On-time delivery*, because it will tell us if we are fulfilling our promises to our customer. A reduction in this measure highlights an obstacle to flow somewhere in the process.

Level 3: Work Cell Critical Success Factors, Goals, and Measures

Once the value stream team has settled on the value stream measures, it must then focus on the work cell. The purpose of the work cell is to produce and deliver 100% quality product, in a smooth flow, on time. Cell actions focus on enabling these three competencies. The team must ask, "What must the cell do very well in order to influence the value stream measures?" These are the cell's critical success factors (CSFs). In order to fulfill customer orders on time, the cell must remove obstacles to flow and focus on kanban and pull systems. Next, the team determines what the goals must be to support each CSF. In order to remove obstacles to flow, the team must reduce batch size, reduce machine downtime, build to order, and eliminate variability. Once the goals are established, the team decides on measures of progress for those goals. For example, managing flow using the day-by-the-hour metric will provide information on batch size, whether we are building to order or focusing on variability. Finally, the five cell measures become the cell's white board metrics kept at the cell by the cell team.

LMEC mapped its goals and measures through three levels. This may vary in companies. Some locations may only have one value stream, so the levels are reduced to two. The important point to remember is that you want the decision makers to have the information when they need it. If the machine worker needs to know when to start a job, then that worker needs the day-by-the-hour metric at hand to make sure that there is not too much or too little product going through the cell at one time. If the value stream team wants to increase throughput through the entire value stream, then it may use the order-to-invoice time as a benchmark to set targets. Table 9.2 offers examples of measures commonly used in value streams and cells.

Measurement Challenges

The preceding LMEC example involved a manufacturing process with well-defined products, actions, and flow. The same alignment mapping process applies to work and work product that is not as well defined. For example, knowledge work, such as product development, report writing, or even month-end closing, can be more difficult to measure, because at first blush, the process and product are more difficult to see. The key is to remember that all work is a process. The first place to start is to map the process itself. A value stream map as described in Chapter 2 will help the team see the process and the associated waste. It will also help to see *what* measures are needed and *where* those measures need to be placed in the process.

It is easier to determine appropriate input and output measures than process measures. Process measures, however, can be the most valuable because they highlight issues as quickly as possible and can trigger timely countermeasures. The type of process also affects the complexity of choosing measures. Production of a physical product is an example of a fairly straightforward process. The goal is to produce a quality product, in a smooth flow, delivered to the customer on time. Quality can be monitored at various points in the process, and rate of production can be tracked periodically throughout the day.

But what if the process is less tangible? An engineering company has identified one value stream whose primary process entails testing specific equipment and writing a collaborative report concerning the results of those tests. The final report undergoes rigorous review, resulting in the customer receiving a report with 100% accuracy. However, it may be at the expense of several rewrites, which constitute excess costs and delays. The challenge becomes how to recognize errors early and identify root causes to prevent reoccurrence. In this case, engineers can use a computer system to track document handoffs as various parts of the report are completed. A field is added into which is typed the reason for the report being returned to another engineer for rework. A histogram highlights the primary sources of problems from the collected data field. From this information, solutions can be implemented to dramatically reduce the need for reworking the document. The key is in recognizing the report as a product and the tasks required to complete the report as a process.

In the preceding example, a meaningful process metric was established by identifying where the risks of problems were in the process. Figure 9.3 presents a measurement selection worksheet that helps identify where the risks are in a process.* The steps to complete this worksheet are simple. The first step is to list everything that can go wrong at various stages of the process. Next, the impact of that problem is identified. For example, it could be that substandard material is delivered to the machine resulting in work stoppage, which possibly delays shipping. The third step on the measurement selections worksheet rates the severity of the impact on a 1–10 scale, with 10 being extremely severe. The severity rating identifies the high-risk parts of the process. These are the points at which control systems should be in place to prevent, or at least to immediately detect, problems. The fourth step defines what can be created to immediately catch or prevent the problem from occurring in the future. Completing this worksheet

---

* This measurement selection worksheet is similar to the failure modes and effects analysis (FMEA) often used in Six Sigma analyses.

NOTE: This tool is designed to help guide the user through selection of the most helpful and meaningful process measures.

PROCESS: *Technical Report Writing*

Step 1: List all potential problems in column *b*.
Step 2: Insert the impact of the problem in column c.
Step 3: Rate the severity of the problem effects in column *d*.
Step 4: For each problem, complete columns *e*, *f*, and *g*.

a	b	c	d	e	f	g
Potential Problem #	What can go wrong in the process?	What is the impact if it happens?	How severe is the effect? (1–10)	What needs to be tracked to prevent errors or defects?	How frequently should processes be checked?	What is the measure?
1	Technical Error	Wrong conclusion can lead to product failure	10	The type and frequency of errors	Each report handoff	# of errors
2	Typos	Lower quality perception leads to dissatisfied customer	7	Frequency of typos	Before each report handoff	# of errors
3	Missed Deadline	Late delivery — unhappy customer; lose customer	9	Progress over time	Weekly	Days to delivery countdown; % completion

Figure 9.3   Measurement selection worksheet.

requires the user to think through all the activities in the process very carefully and question all the controls that are in place.

Action Tracking Logs

A core principle of lean management is to determine the underlying causes of problems and implement solutions to prevent reoccurrence. Underlying causes are not always easy to find with one or even two occurrences. One way to uncover common, or systemic, problems is by using a simple histogram or check sheet. Figure 9.4 illustrates an action tracking chart kept at a work cell that marks how many times shipments were late due to specific reasons. These reasons roll forward onto a tracking sheet where someone is assigned to investigate the cause. It also includes a target date for when the solution will be implemented. Action tracking logs such as these are invaluable in making sure that problems do not reoccur. They also are good for finding trends and systemic problems across value streams or processes by comparing highlighted problems.

Summary

It is very important for decisions to be supported with good data and measures. Sometimes identifying the best measurements is very difficult. To point you in the right direction, consider the decision that needs to be made, as well as the

ISSUES TRACKING: On-Time Delivery

Order #	Order Shipped					Material delivered late	Crimping machine down	Wrong label applied	Wrong material used
	</= CR	1–5 days late	6–10 days late	>10 days late					
1001	X								
1002			X				X		
1003		X				X			
1004		X						X	
1005			X				X		
1006	X								
1007	X								
1008		X							X
1009				X			X		

CR = Customer Requirement Date

ACTION TRACKING

Issue	Start Date	Owner	Due Date		Wk 1	Wk 2	Wk 3	Wk 4	Wk 5	W 6
Material delivered late	1/10/xx	Jane M.	2/01/xx		IP	IP	Late	Late		
Crimping machine down	1/15/xx	Bill S.	3/31/xx		IP	IP	IP	FIN 3/20		
Wrong label applied	2/20/xx	Gary T.	4/30/xx		IP	IP	IP	IP	FIN 4/15	
Wrong material used	2/28/xx	Mary T.	4/30/xx		IP	IP	IP			

IP = In Process
FIN = Finished Date

Figure 9.4 Issues tracking and action tracking sheets.

user of the information. Using a methodical process to think about strategies, goals, and measures at different levels helps to ensure everyone is in agreement and buys in to the measures he or she will use to manage the business. Employees who participate in the alignment process are more likely to feel they "own" the measure and will strive to make decisions to make it work.

Knowledge work processes can be very difficult to measure, but using a tool such as the measurement selection worksheet helps to identify and mitigate risks within the process itself. All work is a process—and all processes can be broken down into activities and steps. Knowledge work is no exception. Once outlined as a process, it is easier to see where quality problems are most likely to occur and identify where controls should be placed.

This chapter has discussed reasons why measurements must change in lean organizations, as well as outlined processes to select and align measures with goals. Performance measurement is a system, however, and selecting measures is one very important factor in the system. Equally important is how these measures are communicated, as well as how these measures impact behavior and decisions. Chapter 10 discusses these facets and helps you evaluate how well your measures support your organization.

Discussion Questions

1. Why is it important to have performance measures in a lean environment? What constitutes a good performance measure?
2. Why does management accounting information need to be different for lean enterprises as compared to traditional organizations?
3. Describe the different behaviors that are motivated by input as compared to output measures.
4. How should you determine what are the most appropriate performance measures to track for effective decision making?
5. What are the main considerations for determining how to actually measure the desired data items?
6. What are the keys to effective measurement alignment? Why does it matter if measures are aligned?
7. Briefly describe the measurement alignment process, including the different levels of measurement.
8. How can an effective measurement system help identify and correct process problems?
9. How do you think you can use the concepts from this chapter to improve your current performance measurement system?

Chapter 10

Measurement and Lean Behavior

How do you know whether the measurements you are currently using to manage your business would be considered lean measures? In other words, does a specific measure guide decisions that meet your goals, and does it do so while adhering to lean principles? These can be tough questions to answer. To do so requires that we revisit the reasons suggested in the previous chapter for *why* we measure.

First, we measure to *support decision making*. We want to provide feedback so that employees can learn whether they are on track or if they need to adjust what they do in order to achieve a different result. We want to identify problems quickly so that they can be resolved before affecting our customers. Putting process measurements in place that quickly and effectively provide feedback and alert us to problems enables employees to have the information they need to make better decisions.

The second reason we measure is to *evaluate outcomes and strategy*. Managers at all levels need to measure the results of processes and actions in order to assign accountability for those results and reward employees for their performance. Measurements are the way we communicate priorities, expectations, and progress. It is essential that the impacts measurements have on decisions be thoughtfully considered before implementation because the wrong measures can have hidden and debilitating effects!

This chapter introduces an assessment tool that will help you determine if the measures you are using are motivating the decisions you want in a lean environment. It will help you to better understand the strengths and weaknesses of your measurements. By the end of this chapter, you should be able to do the following:

- Understand how some traditional measures can motivate nonlean behavior.
- Describe the three attributes of good measurements.
- Use the assessment tool to determine if your measurements are motivating decisions in a lean environment.
- Discuss different ways of using the assessment tool.

Impact of Traditional Measures

Traditional measures support mass manufacturing environments very well because they encourage building inventory in order to drive down unit product cost. The more units produced, the greater number over which to spread fixed costs. The result? Lower cost per unit. In the initial stages of its lean journey, LMEC used a metric common in manufacturing facilities. It was net good pieces or yield, calculated as the volume of production less any loss due to rejects. This is a simple calculation that benchmarks how well the production line is running and how productive it has been. Managers strive to beat this number in successive periods, because this improvement is perceived as positive growth that results in more saleable product, and hence more profit. While the quality measure related to the percentage of good pieces produced is helpful, the other facet of this measure can motivate the wrong behavior. The measure on its own does not relate the increase in production quality to actual sales. It is entirely possible— even probable—that the increased volume is sitting in the warehouse waiting to be sold, and is actually incurring even more storage and handling costs than the savings from increasing quality.

One of the fears of building inventory is the cost burden of warehouse storage and handling that is added to the product. This cost is never actually assigned to the product; rather, it is hidden in shipping and distribution costs. It can be difficult to convince production managers that they should pull back on production so as not to incur these additional costs—especially if managers are measured and rewarded on making product! The following illustration may help explain why it is important to produce product only when there is an order.

> LMEC performed an analysis of warehouse costs. It determined that the cost of utilities, taxes, forklifts, battery chargers, equipment, and people was $500,000 per year. The warehouse racks had 5,000 pallet openings. Therefore, the cost of one pallet opening is $100 per year ($500,000/5,000 pallets). One pallet was configured to hold 10 units of the facility's highest-volume product, with a total product cost per pallet of $50. The average sales price for that pallet was $80, resulting in a $30 profit, or 37.5% return on sales (ROS). But that profit only holds if the product travels straight from the machine line to the delivery truck. What if it is held in inventory for any length of time? Consider the following common scenarios in which finished product is moved from production into the warehouse racks, stored for a period of time, and then sold. The length of storage is indicated by the number of inventory turns, with 1 turn indicating that the pallet was stored for the entire year and 50 indicating that 50 pallets of product were moved in and out of a single pallet opening during 1 year (see Table 10.1).

Only as the inventory turns approach flowing immediately out the dock door does the profit come close to the operating profit of 37.5%. It should also be noted that this example reflects only the costs of storage. What is missing is the

Table 10.1 Inventory Turns Example

Inventory Turns per Year	Total Cost (product cost on one pallet + storage costs)	Profit (Loss) (sales price – total cost)	Return on Sales (profit/sales price)
1	$50 + $100 = $150	$80 – $150 = ($70)	(87.5%)
2	$50 + ($100/2) = $100	$80 – $100 = ($20)	(25.0%)
5	$50 + ($100/5) = $70	$80 – $70 = $10	12.5%
10	$50 + ($100/10) = $60	$80 – $60 = $20	25.0%
20	$50 + ($100/20) = $55	$80 – $55 = $25	31.3%
50	$50 + ($100/50) = $52	$80 – $52 = $28	35.0%

potential cost of obsolescence, damage, excess movement, and invested working capital.

As this warehouse example illustrates, producing units for which there is no sales order inevitably adds cost to the product. Net good pieces as a measurement in production implies that producing quality units is good regardless, even though it can motivate building inventory without orders. Is it good to be able to produce more units? Absolutely! Is the goal to produce more units than we sell? Absolutely not! The goal of a lean system is to produce a quality product at the pull of the customer. There are alternative measures to ensure that you meet that goal. One of the most common is the day-by-hour report. This is a white board or monitor display at the cell that reports how many good units must be produced each hour in order to fill orders for that particular shift. In addition to the targeted production, the actual production is recorded so that it is easy to see whether or not shipments will be met for that shift, or if it is necessary to trigger additional attention and resources to compensate for running behind schedule.

There are other measures used in traditional reporting environments that are not conducive to lean principles. In a standard costing system, key controls used to determine how well the production area is performing are manufacturing variances for material, labor, and overhead. Variances are generally calculated once a month after the books are closed and the financial statements are issued. They compare the actual consumption of material and labor resources with what was expected for the volume produced. Managers are then responsible for investigating reasons for the variances and are held accountable for the result. Overhead variances are much more difficult to interpret, and basically simply inform managers whether or not they produced according to plan. All three of these variances are very sensitive to volume. Producing more units than planned generally results in more favorable variances. Further, manufacturing variances are usually an important component of managers' performance assessment. As a result, there is significant motivation to overproduce, which has been identified as the most egregious of the seven wastes.

Attributes of a Good Measure

You may now be reviewing a list of key measures in your company and wondering whether they are good lean measures. Good question! There are three attributes of a good measure: technical, behavioral, and cultural (Ansari et al., 1996). The following sections explain each attribute.

Technical Attributes

There are two critical questions to ask about any measure: (1) "Does this measure tell me anything about the process?" and (2) "Is this information relevant to a decision?" The technical attribute considers both process understanding and decision relevancy.

Traditional measures focus on functional performance measures, often referred to as responsibility reporting. These measures focus attention on managing people and functions more than on measuring cross-functional processes. In a lean organization, managers understand that operating results are a function of how processes are organized. Chapter 9 discussed input, process, and output measures. Although all are important to successful performance, good process measures are absolutely critical. In traditional measurement systems, most measures compare performance to internal measures (e.g., prior year, budget, forecast). Externally focused customer needs are the primary benchmarks in a lean system. To manage lean organizations, managers need measures that are process focused. Generally, a performance measurement system should aid in the understanding of what causes cost, why unproductive or idle capacity exists, and how the various parts of the value chain are related.

Measures also need to be decision relevant, meaning they must provide information that changes periodically and improves judgment. Older reporting systems are usually riddled with information no longer used to make decisions. Over time, decisions change, decision makers change, and the information relevant for the decision also changes. Periodically, information provided to managers needs to be reviewed to make sure that it is still relevant. In a lean enterprise, where employees seek continuous improvements, the accounting measures can assist work process redesign by identifying non-value-added or unsynchronized activities that do not address customer requirements. Appropriate measures can also lead to better distribution of resources by identifying and monitoring process bottlenecks. Figure 10.1 presents five questions to help you decide if the technical attributes of a measure are sound.

Behavioral Attributes

Behavioral attributes refer to whether measures motivate employee actions that are consistent with strategic objectives. Employees pay attention to measures and

Technical Attribute

Does this measure...

1. provide information that helps to manage cost, quality, or customer service?
2. add to the user's knowledge base?
3. add to the user's understanding of the process?
4. provide information concerning the sources of problems?
5. provide information that is relevant to the decision in question?

Behavioral Attribute

Does this measure...

1. provide information on how well one or more strategic goals are achieved?
2. motivate desired behavior?
3. evaluate the performance of only those employees able to influence the metric?
4. convey clearly to the users how the measure is calculated?
5. convey clearly to the users target expectations?

Cultural Attribute

Does this measure...

1. provide information on process factors affecting customer value?
2. provide information that promotes thinking about the process or value stream as a whole?
3. promote continuous improvement?
4. identify and/or eliminate waste?
5. ensure that employees who make decisions have adequate information?

Figure 10.1 Key questions for the technical, behavioral, and cultural attributes.

focus their efforts on activities accordingly. For example, measuring the percent of defective parts motivates a purchasing agent to select suppliers who have higher-quality products, even if it means a modest increase in cost. If the procurement manager announces that the company instead will more closely monitor the purchase price variance, the likely effect would be for the purchasing agent to negotiate lower costs—perhaps at the expense of quality. The impact of measures on behaviors and decisions is even greater when tied to performance appraisals and incentives.

What a company chooses to measure conveys more to the employee than just the information. Managers establish priorities by selecting certain measures, because by doing so, they communicate to employees what is important to the company. Figure 10.1 presents five questions that provide insight into the behavioral attributes of a measure.

Cultural Attributes

Cultural attributes refer to the beliefs and values embedded in a measure, and measures are symbols that represent mindsets held by members of organizations. For example, the customer value mindset will force a business to consider measures that evaluate safety, quality, delivery, and cost through a customer-focused lens. The mindset of a lean enterprise's employees would not support a measure that encourages overproduction of inventory because it contradicts the flow-and-pull principle. Employees would, however, recognize the value of a measure that encourages efficient use of space (for example, occupancy charge per square foot used) because they would quickly recognize extra space as waste. Figure 10.1 contains questions that help to inform the cultural attribute of a measure.

Assessment

In an ideal situation, a company would not hesitate to completely revamp the performance measurement system in order to support lean strategy. But that is not always a practical solution. Current measures may be embedded in employee performance appraisal systems, bonus schemes, and gain sharing programs. Systems are already designed to collect and report the current information. Changing an entire performance measurement system is costly and can meet with tremendous resistance. Even though the new measure may be considered ideal to those implementing it, the implementation can be very difficult both constructively and politically. Companies with multiple locations face more complex situations that require considerable coordination.

So what can the individual plant managers do to gain a better understanding of the measures in use and whether they support lean principles? It is difficult to develop good measures that consider the three attributes of good measurement and reflect the five principles of lean management. Figure 10.2 depicts the complexity of the process. The questionnaire explained in this chapter and presented in Appendix B will help you to methodically think through a specific measure with respect to the three attributes and five lean principles. The items in the questionnaire were developed in collaboration with managers at LMEC and specifically address each of the three attributes: technical, cultural, and behavioral. So how does the assessment work?

Step 1: Select a specific measurement for assessment.
Step 2: Complete the assessment for the selected measurement. Each attribute has a page divided into two sections. The first section is designed to have the user think through several aspects of a measure, such as how it is measured and used, and who uses the measure. It is important to thoughtfully complete the first section of the attribute assessment. After the user has

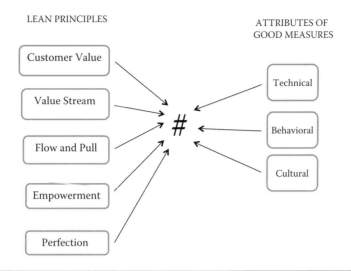

Figure 10.2   Lean principles and attributes of good measures.

considered all these aspects, Section 2 asks the user to rate his or her agreement related to five questions.

Step 3: Average the five scores for each attribute of the measure.

Step 4: Present and discuss the results, and plan how to move forward.

Figure 10.3 illustrates how these two sections work for the technical attribute. Panel A uses selected questions to demonstrate how these questions might be answered for two distinct measures—machine utilization and percent defects. These are actual responses from employees using the assessment. You can easily begin to see how different the results are between the measures. Figures 10.4 and 10.5 demonstrate similar contrasts for the behavioral and cultural measures, respectively.

Once the average scores are computed for each attribute, a summary graph, such as the one in Figure 10.6, reflects the measures' consistency with lean thinking. The graph helps identify strengths and limitations of the measures currently captured in the performance measurement system. Remember, scores closer to 5 indicate the measure is more consistent with the lean philosophy. As an example, the results for inventory turns suggest that the measure is fairly consistent with lean thinking, as reflected in all three attributes. The results for machine utilization, however, indicate that technically the measure has certain benefits, but it is not very consistent with the organization's lean culture and may not motivate decisions and behaviors consistent with lean principles.

This graph is the starting place for discussion. The individual responses behind this graph can be summarized in Excel, which allows for each of the five rating items to inform the discussion. Figure 10.7 shows how scores can be highlighted using Excel functions. Colors can be used to quickly highlight the lowest or highest score. This will help to facilitate discussion on the facets of the measure.

Panel A: Example Questions about the Measure

Example Questions	Machine Utilization	% Defects
T1 Who uses this measurement information?	Managers/supervisors	Cell/VS
T2 What decisions does the measurement inform?	I don't know	Identify systemic quality problems
T4 Is it a functional or process-oriented measure?	Functional	Process
T7 Does this measure relate to product or service quality?	No; maybe indirectly	Yes
T8 Does the measure provide information on the causes of defects?	No	Yes
T9 Does this measure relate to customer service?	If machines are down	Yes

Note: In the question numbers, *T* designates the question as referring to the technical attribute.

Panel B: Assessment Statements about the Measure

Assessment Statement: This measure…	Machine Utilization	% Defects
1. Provides information that helps to manage cost, quality, or customer service.	2	5
2. Adds to the user's knowledge base.	2	5
3. Adds to the user's understanding of the process.	2	5
4. Provides information concerning the sources of problems.	3	3
5. Provides information that is relevant to the decision in question.	3	5
AVERAGE SCORE	2.4	4.6

Figure 10.3   Actual scenario comparison for the technical attribute.

Panel A: Example Questions about the Measure

Example Questions	*Machine Utilization*	*% Defects*
B1 How does this measure relate to employee work or output (e.g., quality or throughput)?	Not directly	Directly—Motivates finding causes of quality problems
B2 How does this measure relate to the strategic goals of my facility?	Assures having product to sell when needed	Supports making a quality product
B3 Where does the measure focus attention?	Keeping machines up	Customer value
B4 What behavior does it actually motivate?	Produce inventory	Make quality product
B10 Is there a reward for goal achievement? If so, what is the reward?	No—Keep job	Affects profit-sharing contribution

Note: In the question numbers, *B* designates the question as referring to the behavioral attribute.

Panel B: Assessment Statements about the Measure

Assessment Statement: *This measure…*	*Machine Utilization*	*% Defects*
1. Provides information on how well we are achieving one or more strategic goals.	1	5
2. Motivates desired behavior.	2	5
3. Is used to evaluate the performance of employees able to effect change in the metric.	2	5
4. Conveys clearly to the users how the measure is calculated.	4	5
5. Conveys clearly to the users target expectations.	4	5
AVERAGE SCORE	2.6	5

Figure 10.4   Actual scenario comparison for the behavioral attribute.

Panel A: Example Questions about the Measure

Example Questions	*Machine Utilization*	*% Defects*
C3 Does this measure reflect value as defined from the customer's viewpoint?	No	Yes
C4 Does this measure promote thinking about the entire value stream or does it focus on an individual department?	No—Just production, maybe maintenance	Yes
C6 Does this measure encourage minimizing inventory or building inventory?	Building inventory	Minimizing inventory
C7 Does this measure provide adequate information to the people making the decision?	No	Yes
C8 Does this measure promote continuous improvement at the cell or value stream level?	Limited	Yes

Note: In the question numbers, *C* designates the question as referring to the cultural attribute.

Panel B: Assessment Statements about the Measure

Assessment Statement: *This measure . . .*	*Machine Utilization*	*% Defects*
1. Provides information on process factors affecting customer value.	1	5
2. Provides information that promotes thinking about the process or value stream as a whole.	1	4
3. Promotes continuous improvement as well as identification and elimination of waste.	3	5
4. Ensures that employees who make decisions are well-informed and have adequate information to make decisions.	1	5
5. Ensures that employees who make decisions have adequate information.	4	5
AVERAGE SCORE	2.0	4.8

Figure 10.5   Actual scenario comparison for the cultural attribute.

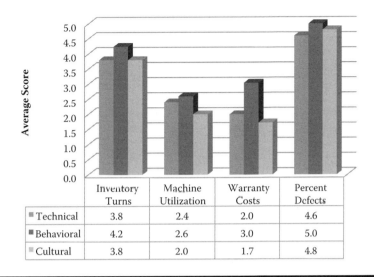

	Inventory Turns	Machine Utilization	Warranty Costs	Percent Defects
■ Technical	3.8	2.4	2.0	4.6
■ Behavioral	4.2	2.6	3.0	5.0
▨ Cultural	3.8	2.0	1.7	4.8

Figure 10.6   Assessment results.

Summary

Measurement is very important in any organization. Measures provide direction and feedback, guide decisions, monitor progress, and trigger actions. Selecting the correct measures may not be easy, but it is absolutely critical for successful lean operations. The process described in this chapter leads employees through a series of questions to stimulate their thinking about a measure's desired qualities and the information the measure provides. As a result, employees may identify redundancies in the measures. Streamlining the performance measurement set facilitates a more accurate and timely evaluation of performance. Careful analysis of your measures may also highlight their limitations. By directing attention to the measure's characteristics and then assessing the measurement using consistent criteria, employees should realize both the strengths and weaknesses in the measure, including the calculation's accuracy, the message it conveys to employees, and its alignment with the corporate mindset. This knowledge facilitates improvements in your performance measurement system by revealing measures that need tweaking to be more consistent with desired attributes.

Discussion Questions

1. What are some of the most critical reasons for taking an assessment of your current performance measurement system?
2. Explain why some traditional measures are not appropriate in a lean environment.

Technical

			Inventory Turns	Machine Utilization	Warranty Costs	Percent Defects
Q1.	This measure provides information that helps to manage cost, quality, and/or customer service.		5.00	2.00	4.00	5.00
Q2.	This measure adds to the user's knowledge base.		4.00	2.00	4.00	5.00
Q3.	This measure adds to the user's understanding of the process.		3.00	2.00	2.00	5.00
Q4.	This measure provides information concerning the sources of the problems.		1.00	3.00	1.00	3.00
Q5.	This measure provides information that is relevant to the decision in question.		4.00	3.00	3.00	5.00
	Overall Assessment		**3.40**	**2.40**	**2.80**	**4.60**

Behavioral

			Inventory Turns	Machine Utilization	Warranty Costs	Percent Defects
Q1.	This measure provides information on how well one or more strategic goals are achieved.		4.00	1.00	3.00	5.00
Q2.	This measure motivates desired behavior.		4.20	2.00	3.00	5.00
Q3.	This measure evaluates the performance of only those employees able to effect change in the metric.		4.00	2.00	1.00	5.00
Q4.	This measure conveys clearly to the users how the measure is calculated.		4.00	4.00	4.00	5.00
Q5.	This measure conveys clearly to the users target expectations.		5.00	4.00	4.00	5.00
	Overall Assessment		**4.24**	**2.60**	**3.00**	**5.00**

Cultural

			Inventory Turns	Machine Utilization	Warranty Costs	Percent Defects
Q1.	This measure provides information on process factors affecting customer value.		4.00	1.00	3.00	5.00
Q2.	This measure provides information that promotes thinking about the process or value stream as a whole.		4.00	1.00	4.00	4.00
Q3.	This measure promotes continuous improvement.		3.80	3.00	4.00	5.00
Q4.	This measure identifies and/or eliminates waste.		3.20	1.00	4.00	5.00
Q5.	This measure ensures that employees who make decisions have adequate information.		4.00	4.00	3.00	5.00
	Overall Assessment		**3.80**	**2.00**	**3.60**	**4.80**

Figure 10.7   Actual assessment data.

3. Name and describe the three attributes of a good performance measurement system. Why are these important? Are there other attributes that should be considered as well?

4. Who will benefit most from an assessment of your performance measurement system and why?

5. What do you think is the most critical piece of the metric assessment process?

6. Why do you think people are resistant to evaluating their performance measurement system with the objective of improving it?
7. How long has it been since your company has done a critical assessment of its performance measurement system? How often do you think it should be reevaluated?

Reference

Ansari, S., J. Bell, T. Klammer, and C. Lawrence. 1996. *Strategy and management accounting*. Houghton Mifflin, Boston, MA.

CONTROLS AND TRANSITION

Chapter 11

Leaning Accounting Processes

As discussed in the introduction to this workbook, there is an important distinction between lean accounting and accounting for lean. Prior chapters on performance measurements, value stream costing, decision making, lean planning, and inventory and capacity management focused on the latter perspective—accounting for lean organizations. This is an important and challenging responsibility, requiring accountants to critically consider how to best fulfill the information needs of a lean entity. However, in this chapter, our focus is on lean accounting—applying lean principles to improve accounting processes.

All accounting processes need to be examined to unearth hidden improvement opportunities. As you review your own processes, you will likely discover that some activities and transactions are no longer needed because lean operations no longer require certain information. While many activities and transactions produce valuable information, they may still be ripe for improvement opportunities. In this chapter, we outline methods that will help you sift through your accounting processes to identify areas of opportunity, prioritize these areas, and develop an action plan.

At the end of this chapter, you should be able to do the following:

- Identify activities and transactions that can be eliminated or streamlined.
- Better understand how information is used by your internal customer.
- Prioritize improvement opportunities for the most benefit.
- Prepare an action plan to get started.

Eliminate or Improve?

The most critical point to remember is that no accounting activity can be eliminated without thoughtful consideration of all its ramifications. This means that you must carefully analyze what information is provided, to whom it is provided, and how it is used. Prematurely eliminating information can leave users without the tools they need to make decisions and can result in confusion and loss of control. We have identified six steps that will help you sift through your accounting processes to decide which activities are ready to eliminate or streamline: (1) list all accounting processes and activities, (2) quantify the time and resources consumed by these activities, (3) perform a customer value analysis for each activity, (4) consider the cost and impact of changing an activity, (5) select the activity or activities for change, and (6) prepare an action plan to make changes to the activity. These steps are outlined in Table 11.1 and discussed below.

Step 1: List All Accounting Processes and Activities

LMEC was faced with the decision of where to begin. The task seemed daunting for several reasons. First, the sheer volume of activities performed by the accounting department seemed overwhelming. In addition, some tasks are very complex and require considerable information from other departments. Most of the activities drove reporting, but there are other activities that the controller considered ongoing maintenance and record keeping. What it all boiled down to was that the controller didn't know where to start! She didn't know which activity should start their journey toward leaner accounting processes.

The controller found that she had to get an overview of the departmental processes and activities before she was comfortable choosing the first activity to tackle. Just as the first step for a value stream team is to map the value stream (discussed in Chapter 2), a visual was needed to provide a snapshot of all the activities performed by the accounting department so she could see the opportunities more clearly. The example we use describes and outlines this selection process.

The first step is to compile a list of all your accounting activities and processes. Our example, which is provided in the first column of Table 11.2, identifies two general accounting processes (inventory and payroll), and the individual activities that support those processes. The number of activities and the amount of detail you want to examine depend on the complexities of your organization and accounting system.

Step 2: Quantify Time and Resources

After identifying activities, estimate the amount of time it takes to perform each of the tasks within that activity. Start with the accounting department and identify any employee involved in the activity. Be sure to consider areas outside of accounting that may also have employees spending time and resources on the tasks. For example, time card processing requires that production employees record their time, supervisors sign off on each card, and production assistants gather and deliver the time cards to the payroll clerk in accounting. It is

Table 11.1   Six Steps to Selecting and Planning Lean Improvements in Accounting Activities

Step 1: List all accounting processes and activities	1.1 What are all the major accounting processes? 1.2 What are all the activities performed in each process?
Step 2: Quantify the time and resources consumed by these activities	2.1 Who performs each activity in accounting? 2.2 Are people in other departments also involved in the activity? 2.3 How much time is spent by each person? 2.4 How frequently is the activity performed? 2.5 What other resources are consumed? Contract labor? Machine downtime? Equipment? 2.6 Which activities consume the most resources?
Step 3: Perform a customer value analysis for each activity	3.1 Who uses the information? 3.2 What decisions are made with the information? 3.3 How is it used? 3.4 Are there activities where users no longer use the information? 3.5 Why don't they use it? Has the decision changed? Has the decision gone away? If this activity was eliminated, would anyone miss the information? 3.6 Is this information currently available in lean operations? 3.7 If not, will it be available when lean is fully implemented? 3.8 Which activities will not have lean alternatives? Can they be streamlined?
Step 4: Consider the cost and impact of change	Of one activity: 4.1 Does this activity require a simple change that can be implemented quickly and at no cost? 4.2 How much employee time will it take to plan and implement a change in this activity? 4.3 Is it likely that there will be additional costs or investment, such as equipment or software? 4.4 What is the impact of the change on the information's customer? 4.5 What is the impact on quality of information?
Step 5: Select the activity or activities for change	5.1 Which activity or activities are the best ones to start the continuous improvement process? • Is it the quickest or costless? • Will it have the most impact? • Does it save resources? • Will it impact other departments?

continued

Table 11.1 (continued)   Six Steps to Selecting and Planning Lean Improvements in Accounting Activities

Step 6: Prepare an action plan	Of one activity:
	6.1 What is the current state of the process?
	6.2 What is the ideal state?
	6.3 What do we have to do to fill the gap?
	6.4 Are there obstacles to filling the gap? If so, what are they? How can they be overcome? What countermeasures should be in place?
	6.5 Who needs to be involved?
	6.6 When will this be completed? What does it look like in 3, 6, 9, and 12 months?
	6.7 What are the next steps?

important that your time estimate takes into account everyone involved in the entire process.

In addition to time, activities may consume other resources, such as supplies and equipment. It is not necessary at this point to spend resources to map these activities in detail. The purpose of this step is to get a broad picture of resource consumption. This will help to prioritize improvement opportunities. Once activities are selected for further analysis, then resources can be assigned to analyze the processes more thoroughly.

After all of the accounting activities are listed and the resources from each department are estimated and totaled, it will be easier to see where efforts are focused and which activities consume the most resources. Table 11.2 provides an example of the type of information you will want to collect. The last column shows a resource score, which represents the magnitude of resource usage for each activity. There are different ways to assign the resource score to the individual activities. In our example, we used a scale of 1 to 10, with 10 being the most resource usage by an activity and 1 being the least. You could also use a percentage of resource usage. The score assigned is meant to be a relatively straightforward estimation of resource usage, determined with the input of process owners and supervisors. It is generally not necessary to expend considerable effort in obtaining specific, detailed data. This score is one of several inputs that will help you identify the greatest opportunities.

Step 3: Perform a Customer Value Analysis

The purpose of the customer value analysis (CVA) is to carefully consider how and if the information provided by an activity is currently used by your customer (generally this is an internal customer), and whether or not it is relevant in a lean environment. If the activity continues to be relevant and useful, there may be an opportunity to streamline and improve the information gathering and delivery.

Table 11.2 Activity Resources Detail

Activity	Calculation	Quantity of Time and Resources (hours)			Annual Total Hours	Other Resource	Resource Score[a]
		Accounting	Production	Warehouse			
Inventory Processes							
Bill of materials maintenance (monthly)	Accounting: 1 person × 10 h/wk	10/wk			520		8
Physical inventory (annual)	Accounting: 5 people × 30 hours Production/warehouse: 20 people × 12 h	150/yr	120/yr	120/yr	390	24 h machine downtime	9
Periodic inventory (monthly)	Accounting: 1 person × 3 h Production: 1 person × 1 h	3/mo	1/mo		48		3
Perpetual inventory reconciliation (monthly)	Accounting: 1 person × 6 h	6/mo			72		4
Payroll Processing							
Time card processing (weekly)	Accounting: 1 person × 16 h/wk	16/wk			832		10
Discrepancy reconciliation (weekly)	Accounting: 1 person × 6 h	6/wk			312		6
Remittances (e.g., check, auto pay) (weekly)	Accounting: 1 person × 4 h	4/wk			208		3
Tax report preparation (quarterly)	Accounting: 1 person × 3 h	3/qtr			12		2

[a] Resource score: Score each activity on a scale of 1–10 indicating the degree of time and resources consumed by the activity, with 1 being the least amount of resource usage and 10 being the most.

If the information is no longer useful, then it should be eliminated. The biggest potential pitfall in the CVA—and the one that will cause major problems down the road—is to overlook someone up- or downstream who uses the reported information. This oversight can lead to a major gap in information dissemination that may negatively impact not only reporting accuracy, but also operating decisions. The CVA needs to be performed by team members most familiar with the process to help ensure a thorough CVA.

Table 11.3 shows a partial CVA for the bill of materials maintenance activity. The first column lists everyone who uses any information provided by the bill of materials. The second column explains how the information is used. *Make sure that all users and uses of the information are listed!* The third column determines whether or not the information is currently available in lean operations. Finally, the last column designates if the information will be available once lean practices are more fully implemented or if it is unnecessary. In this example, four users were identified along with how they use the information. The information used by Joe to see how parts are produced and packed is available another way—through standard operating procedures (SOPs). Mary, from the purchasing department, uses the bill of materials to know how much material to order. Right now, there is no other way for her to get that information. However, once production has implemented visual kanbans that trigger purchase orders, she will no longer

Table 11.3 Customer Value Analysis for the Bill of Materials Maintenance Activity

Activity: Bill of materials maintenance Resource score = 8			
Who Uses This Information?	*Why/ How Is It Used?*	*Is This Information Currently Available in Lean Operations?*	*Will the Information Be Available or Necessary in Future Lean Operations?*
Joe—production supervisor	See how part is produced and packed	Yes—SOPs at the cell	n/a
Mary— purchasing agent	See how much to order	No	Yes—Visual kanbans will signal when to purchase more materials
Joe—production supervisor	Schedule people	Not needed because cell team schedules its own work schedules	n/a
Teresa— accountant	Value product cost per unit for financial statements	Not needed for decisions anymore; value stream costing used instead with only material tracked in perpetual inventory	n/a

need the bill of materials. The last two users, Joe and Teresa, no longer need the information.

Step 4: Consider the Cost and Impact of Change

At this point, it is likely that you have a good idea which of your accounting activities you are ready to tackle. Chances are good that as you were performing the customer value analysis, you found some information that was no longer needed or used by your customer. You may also have discovered tasks where the information is already available elsewhere. These activities and tasks are prime candidates to eliminate first. The good news is that these changes eliminate waste created by redundant activities and require no cost to implement!

Now that you have grabbed the low-hanging fruit, the remainder of the activities can be placed into two categories. One requires implementation of additional lean practices that provide required information before the activity can be eliminated. The other includes activities that can be analyzed and streamlined by removing process waste. But before you can jump in and start the work, there are two factors to consider as you select the first set of activities to tackle. You must consider the amount of investment in time and resources to analyze, plan, and implement changes in a specific activity. Can the project be completed in a relatively short amount of time at little cost? Or will it take 10–12 months to complete? Does it also have an investment in software? Does the project require people from different departments to participate in the analysis and planning? In other words, what is the cost of the change for the activity? A second consideration is the impact of the change. It is important to first consider what type of impact, if any, it will have on the user of the information. If the customer value analysis was thoroughly and thoughtfully considered, there should be no negative user impact; in fact, there should actually be a positive impact because the user will not need to sift through redundant or unnecessary information.

Step 5: Select the Activity or Activities for Change

Steps 2 to 4 help you to explicitly consider the cost of current activities, their value to customers, as well as the cost and impact of making changes. Now it is time to use this information and decide which activities are the best ones to begin the improvement process. It may be an activity that can be eliminated immediately because a customer no longer needs the information. It could be an easy change that will not take long and is costless to implement. Or it could be a very cumbersome process that will take time to analyze and change, but the impact of that change will not only save resources, but also greatly improve the relevancy of the information to the customer. Having carefully walked through the activity detail and the customer value analysis, you now understand the activities better and can make a better decision.

Step 6: Prepare an Action Plan

You are now ready to form an action plan for each continuous improvement project. The CVA in Table 11.3 highlighted that some of the information is no longer needed, some of the information is already being prepared, and only one lean practice needs to be implemented before all the information provided by the bill of materials is readily available for all its intended users. The next step is to prepare an action plan for the bill of materials maintenance activity. Figure 11.1 illustrates the contents of a completed action plan for our bill of materials example.

The action plan is really the initial planning document. It helps you to gain an overview of purpose, team membership, general timeline, and first few steps to get started. The four-block portion of the action plan documents the current state of the activity, summarizes what it would look like in its future state, identifies any obstacles the team may encounter to make changes, and provides ideas on how to overcome potential roadblocks and challenges. This snapshot will help you to select the best employees for the improvement team. Remember to include representatives from any department that is involved in the activity or that could potentially contribute to the solution. For example, one obstacle identified in the example was that it may be hard to visualize how the kanban would work. As a result, it may be useful to include people who are experts in design, such as marketing and design engineering. Even though these employees are not directly affected by the bill of materials change, they possess talents that may contribute to developing an innovative visual solution.

LEAN IN ACTION 11.1: STREAMLINING PAYROLL PROCESSING

Before LMEC transitioned to lean, there were 18 labor categories on the production floor based on job function and skill level. Labor variances were calculated and provided for each of these categories every month—and the supervisors were required to explain material differences. The production lines were then reorganized into production cells and machine operators began to cross-train on all the machines in their cell. As a result, the number of labor categories was reduced to two categories and labor variances were no longer calculated. This meant significant time savings for accounting personnel and supervisors. One year later, LMEC ceased to keep track of the number of hours worked by each employee. Instead, the payroll system was programmed to assume 40 hours per week. The supervisor maintained a payroll adjustment sheet that recorded when workers took time off or worked overtime. For example, "Joe Price left two hours early for an appointment." Or "Tammy Smith worked 1.5 hours overtime." Payroll could now be processed in a very short amount of time and that time could be spent on more value-added analyses.

Action Plan

Activity: *Bill of Materials Maintenance*

What needs to be in place in . . .

3 mos?	Project Plan in place, data collected, kanban designed.
6 mos?	Be ready to test.
9 mos?	Kanban running successfully.
12 mos?	Ready to eliminate Bill of Material.

Who needs to be involved in the process?

Ann B., Purchasing Supv.	Adam W., Purchasing
Karen C., Purchasing	Zack K., Prod. Supv.
Tom D., Cell A Lead	Sally T., Marketing
Bruce B., VS Mgr	Gary W., Industrial Eng.

Current State *What do we do now? Date:*	Future State *Ideally, what could it be? Date:*
Lean processes in place except for kanbans to signal purchasing.	Bill of Material not required. Lean processes fill information needs for purchasing, labor scheduling, and packaging.
Obstacles & Challenges	**How to Overcome**
Number of vendors and part numbers will make it hard to visualize.	Visit and see what others are doing; involve people who design as their job, such as marketing and design engineers.

What are the first steps?

1. Organize cross-functional team
2. Enlist champion in management
3. Schedule first meeting
4. Prepare project plan

Figure 11.1   Action plan to eliminate or streamline activity.

The next planning step is to draft a broad timeline with general milestones. This establishes flexible boundaries for the team and helps them visualize project expectations. Once the team meets and begins to delve into the improvement process, they will refine these milestones and use appropriate project tools, such as Gantt charts and A3's, to help the team stay on track. Along with the timeline, the first steps that need to be performed should be clearly spelled out.

Summary

The role of internal reporting is to provide useful information for appropriate decision making. In a lean environment, decisions and information needs change. As accounting practices adapt new, lean reporting mechanisms, some traditional activities are no longer needed. Careful, methodical analysis will help identify activities and reporting that are no longer needed, as well as activities that can be streamlined. You should abide by two rules as you proceed on your journey to leaner accounting processes:

Rule 1: Never eliminate any reporting until the entire activity has been thoroughly investigated.
Rule 2: Make sure that all information users are considered in your analysis.

Methodically and carefully working through the activity resource detail and customer value analysis will ensure that no user goes without necessary information.

Trim off the easy fruit first—it will help you to see the core of the improvement opportunities. As you choose more involved improvements, consider the magnitude of the resources currently consumed in the activity, as well as the potential costs of analyzing, planning, and implementing solutions. Make sure that all processes are in place and working smoothly before eliminating any reporting. This may mean parallel reports for a period until you are confident that the processes are working smoothly.

Finally, just as lean processes result in huge productivity and quality gains in production, you can expect to see similar improvements in the accounting processes as well. As waste is uncovered in redundant and obsolete tasks and activities, and more efficient reporting is implemented, employee efforts can be reassigned to analysis activities and supporting value stream teams. Accountants will have more time to help drive improvements through value-added analysis and reporting.

Discussion Questions

1. How does "lean accounting" differ from "accounting for lean"? Which of the two is easiest to apply and why?
2. What are the most important factors in determining how to improve/streamline your accounting practices?
3. Explain how to prioritize your improvement efforts for your accounting activities.
4. What is the purpose of the Customer Value Analysis? Why is it necessary?
5. What are some of the accounting processes that are generally ripe for improvement—the proverbial "low-hanging fruit"?
6. Explain how the Action Plan is developed and how responsibility for it is determined.
7. How often do you examine your accounting processes for improvement opportunities?
8. How committed is your accounting staff to continuous improvement in their own work?
9. What accounting processes would you like to see improved in your facility?

Chapter 12

Transitioning to a Lean Accounting Reporting System

You have arrived at our final chapter. We have discussed the many different applications and concepts of lean accounting, but we have not yet discussed the actual transition to a new system of reporting. I'm sure you are wondering how organizations actually make the transition from a standard costing system to a more relevant, lean reporting system. Is it really possible? What real benefits come from such a dramatic change? What challenges have others faced? If this is truly a better accounting system, why haven't more organizations embraced it? If I am a single plant in a large corporation, will I be able to still comply with corporate reporting? What issues will I face with the external auditors? How will I make decisions without discrete tracking of all of my individual product costs? We will try to address all of those questions and more in this chapter. Of course, every organization has a different culture and organizational structure. They also vary in complexity and size. We cannot prescribe customized transitions, but from the knowledge gleaned from our research and personal experiences, we can discuss some general guidelines on changing your internal reporting system. After reading this chapter you should have a clearer understanding of the following:

- Basic environmental characteristics required for making a transition to lean accounting.
- The steps and keys to making a successful accounting reporting transition.
- The potential obstacles that must be overcome in order to make the transition to lean accounting.
- The expected benefits from your new reporting system.

Preparing to Transition Your Accounting System

Because of the varied environments of companies and their different stages of lean applications, there is no "cookie cutter" approach to implementing a lean accounting system. It is sometimes difficult to know if and when you are ready to change your internal reporting system to a more relevant system that supports your lean operations. You need a better reporting system to help evaluate your lean operations, but it is not very feasible to transition from your standard costing system until certain lean foundations are in place. For example, if you want to report by value streams (i.e., use value stream costing), you must be organized into value streams. Lean thinking and pockets of lean should be evident throughout your organization. Changing something as traditional as the internal reporting system is a monumental event, and the workforce must be in an accepting, continuous improvement mindset for such change to occur without strong resistance.

Without a company-wide commitment to lean and proper training in lean concepts, revamping your accounting system is probably inappropriate. Before lean accounting can be adopted effectively, accountants should be privy to lean thinking. They should have been included in lean events, such as being members of continuous improvement teams and participants of kaizen events both on the shop floor and in their own processes. If they are not involved with strategic improvement changes throughout the organization, including the finance department, they are not likely to understand or support the need for change in their information reporting methods.

Changing your accounting system is not the first step of implementing lean that you want to take, but neither should it be the last. Typically, accounting systems are used for financial and operational control of the business. Substitute controls must be in place before the traditional system can be eliminated. A lean company no longer requires accounting reports to understand if their processes are under control and operating as intended. Standardization of processes, flow of operations, and kanban pull systems all provide the visual information necessary to assess the effectiveness of current performance, replacing the need for variance analysis and adherence to predesigned budgeted benchmarks. Processes and inventories in this environment are generally stable and inventories low, making some of the external requirements for a standard costing system obsolete. Yet, it is not necessarily easy to predict the proper timing for making substantial changes to your accounting system. You don't want to lose control and create havoc in your operations by changing your reporting system too soon, but you also don't want your accounting system to be a roadblock for lean implementations either.

It would be nearly impossible for an organization to develop a lean culture without the support of top management. Ideally, top management would also encourage a change in the accounting system to support lean operations, but this unfortunately is not always the case. Many administrators or personnel in the corporate offices do not understand the dissonance created with traditional costing methods in a lean environment. Thus, they see no need to change a system with which they are comfortable and has been serving them seemingly successfully for many years. It may be your responsibility to educate them about the inaccuracies and motivational behaviors that standard costs and variances create. They should also be forewarned about the negative effects that will show up on the profit and loss (P&L) statement as inventories are reduced and obsolete inventory is uncovered. Generally, top management is accepting of any changes that will better serve the customer and maintain shareholder confidence. You may need to demonstrate that lean accounting is more customer focused, more accurate, and more in line with lean principles. As changes are made to your reporting system, be sure to inform corporate (CFOs and CEOs) of those changes and keep them involved in the process as much as possible. The stronger the commitment from top management to revamping your internal reporting system, the more likely will be its overall acceptance and success.

There is not anything anti-generally accepted accounting principles (GAAP) in lean accounting. If anything, a lean accounting system should be more accurate than a traditional costing system because you are valuing inventory with more direct costs, rather than allocations. But because this is a change to what has been done in the past, your external auditors need to be involved in the change. They need to understand the new system and be on board with changes from the start. The only real issue that should create external reporting concern is the valuation of inventory. If inventory is low or stable, then inventory reporting changes are minimal and the issues of valuing inventory are minor. When inventories are still relatively large or highly fluctuating, the auditors may have more angst about the ability for lean accounting methods to correctly value inventories. It may not be feasible to change your internal reporting system until your inventories are stable and aligned with lean thinking. Auditors are generally not comfortable with a lean accounting inventory valuation approach until inventory turns are over 12 a year. However, for some firms whose products take considerable time to build, acceptable inventory turns may be just over six or even less, as long as operations and inventories are relatively stable. Regardless, if you have kept the auditors informed of any changes and if the auditors are familiar with lean principles, they will be more supportive and have a better understanding of how lean accounting can be used effectively to meet GAAP standards for inventory valuation.

Steps for Making the Accounting Transition

In this section we will list some general guidelines for the actual accounting transition process. Of course, every organization has its own unique environment, and it must consider the ramifications of each step in transitioning its accounting system.

Step 1: Identify Value Streams and Associated Costs

Before you can consider implementing lean accounting or value stream costing, you must have identified your value streams, and ideally have organized operations into their appropriate value streams. When value streams are in place, you will want to try to assign all of your product costs to an individual value stream. This includes all value stream costs: materials, people, machines, space, shipping, marketing, and other overhead costs. In Chapter 2, we discussed some of the value stream cost assignment issues. It may initially appear relatively easy to identify the product costs that belong to each value stream, since most of these costs are directly traceable to the individual value stream. However, even directly traceable costs can create some assignment issues. For example, each of your employees will need to be assigned to a specific value stream. The traditionally defined direct labor may be easily assignable. But you have engineers, accountants, sales and marketing personnel, and IT specialists that all contribute to value stream costs. Most of these support people are accustomed to working in their own department, and may resent reporting to a value stream and a value stream leader. Further, some of these employees may be servicing more than one value stream. These are complications that must be resolved if you are going to track costs by value streams. You can see how critical it is to first make sure that everyone understands why you should organize your accounting system by value streams, and how this fits with the strategic objectives of your lean organization. The employees must also feel that their role remains vital within the value stream so they do not feel diminished in any way. As to those employees that service several value streams, there are different approaches you can take to assign their costs. For example, if you have six engineers that work on three different value streams, you may assign two engineers per value stream so that engineering costs are spread fairly. Sometimes sales and marketing service all products. If this is the case in your organization, these costs can be assigned either to a general plant value stream or to a sales and marketing value stream—whatever works best for you.

You know by now that allocation of costs in a lean accounting system is to be avoided if at all possible. However, since some machines and people create costs for multiple value streams, it may be necessary to have some allocation scheme in place for these monuments until they can be eliminated. Whatever allocation method you use should motivate behavior that is appropriate for a lean environment and your organization. Most of the time that is not the traditional allocation scheme of machine or labor hours worked. Many companies allocate these monument costs per the portion of plant square footage the value stream occupies. So if a value stream uses 20% of the total floor space available, it would receive 20% of the monument costs. This motivates value stream leaders to improve the performance of their value stream through process improvements that reduce their footprints. It is likely that some floor space will be unoccupied. Thus, not all of the monument costs will be allocated. Instead, these leftover costs will be collected in a separate column on the plain English P&L for plant-wide costs. This approach is helpful in identifying unused capacity. Another method of assigning costs that works well for machine monuments is to use actual machine time used by each value stream.

There are some general plant costs that are necessary, but not traceable to any individual value streams. Employees that fit this description are the plant manager, vice president of operations, CEO, controller, IT specialist, and director of human resources. There may also be insurance costs, plant depreciation, taxes, and corporate allocations that are not traceable to individual value streams. Generally, these types of costs are combined into a general plant value stream (or "sustaining" costs) and not allocated. It is inappropriate to judge the performance of a value stream by costs over which they have no control.

Step 2: Determine Appropriate Method for Valuing Inventory

There are two primary concerns in switching to a lean accounting system: the first is that the inventories are properly valued for the external financial reports, and the second is that there is adequate information for decision making. If inventories are low and stable, their valuation is relatively simple, primarily because any month-to-month adjustments are immaterial. That doesn't mean that you don't need to have a system in place to adequately value your inventory, however. Most lean organizations continue to track materials costs, since these are direct, variable costs and relatively easy transactions to trace. However, inventory conversion costs usually have to be estimated at month end or whatever reporting period you are compiling. Most companies will have a history of their product costs under a traditional costing system. At the time of transition, you can examine the historical relationships of conversion costs to material costs. Depending upon the level of information you want, you may separate the conversion costs into labor and overhead—or bundle these costs together. Regardless, if the relationships between conversion costs and materials have stayed relatively the same for your inventories over a two- or three-year time period, then you can continue to use those relationships in valuing your inventory. For example, if conversion costs have historically been 25% of materials costs, and inventory costs for materials are $100,000 at the end of the period, you would add $25,000 to your inventory cost and show a total of $125,000 on your balance sheet as inventory. (See Chapter 5 for more detailed examples of inventory valuations.)

It is important to separate out your work-in-process (WIP) and finished goods inventory, because the relationships will be different. WIPs will likely have a higher proportion of material costs, since for most processes, the majority of the material costs are added at the beginning of the process and the conversion costs are added throughout the operations. If your organization is typical, materials will represent the majority of costs, so if you account for actual material costs and then make your best approximate adjustment for conversion costs, you have met the materiality requirements for inventory valuation. This is especially true if your inventories are relatively stable. Even though this estimation process may feel uncomfortable initially, it is likely that it is at least as accurate as the traditional system that pretends to have an accurate inventory calculation, even though it is determined through the arbitrary allocation of often outdated and inaccurate overhead rates.

We have observed other acceptable methods in practice for valuing inventories. Some companies continue to track labor hours per specific product lines, even though they do not assign a dollar value to those labor hours. If you know how many labor hours are left in inventory, you can assign a rate for conversion costs related to those labor hours and add it to your material costs to determine your ending inventories. Again, the rates and relationships would need to be based on historical patterns that have been relatively stable. One company we have observed builds large machines that take more than six weeks to complete. Thus, they always have substantial work in process, although it is generally stable. They use Yamazumi boards to track the completion of their work. Yamazumi boards are visual cycle-time depictions of the work that has been completed for each process and the related takt time for each task (see Chapter 5). At the end of the reporting period, the accountant goes to the shop floor and looks at the Yamazumi boards to determine the stage of completion of each machine. There is an already established approximate conversion cost to build each machine, and the inventory value is the percentage of completion times the building cost for each machine. It takes just minutes to make this inventory calculation for conversion costs.

When the ending inventory figure is determined, the accountants make an adjusting journal entry to update the balance sheet inventory figure for conversion costs from the previously reported amount. For those of you who can remember your managerial accounting training, this is similar to the periodic method of accounting for inventory, rather than the perpetual method. All conversion product costs during the month are expensed through the P&L statements, and the inventory is not adjusted until the end of the reporting period. As inventory decreases, conversion costs will be moved from the balance sheet to the P&L, and vice versa—as inventory increases, conversion costs are moved from the P&L to the balance sheet. Remember that material costs are generally updated perpetually, so no end-of-period adjustment needs to be made for them.

Step 3: Identify the Types of Accounting Reports That Are Necessary

Lean is well known for its visual management. If you want people to perform well, they must know how well they are meeting expectations, and if they aren't, they want to know how they can improve. If you hide performance results in computers that have limited or complex access, then employees never get a real sense of how they are performing their jobs. By selecting a few critical key measures that are tied to your strategic objectives and posting them where everyone can easily see the results, there are no excuses and no surprises relative to expected performance. Most lean companies will have very visible performance measures on the shop floor that show day-by-the-hour production (or whatever time frame fits your defined takt time), first time through, on-time delivery, and reportable incidences, or other similar key measures related to safety, quality, delivery, and cost.

Lean companies are also encouraged to develop some type of weekly score sheet that tabulates the performance results from the past week and compares them to prior weeks, as well as forecasted future objectives. A score sheet that has become popular among lean accounting organizations is the box score, which was developed by Brian Maskell. The box score has three key areas: operational, capacity, and financial. A few operational and financial key measures are selected and tracked. Understanding and utilizing capacity is key to lean, so it is a category by itself that reflects weekly (or monthly) productive, nonproductive, and available capacity. Capacity measures are often overlooked in traditional performance measurements systems. The box score was introduced in Chapter 3.

The P&L format for a company that is reporting by value stream is different than the traditional P&L. It is often referred to as a plain English P&L because of its straightforward presentation. On the plain English P&L, there are no variances shown, nor is there a general category of cost of goods sold that lumps all production costs together and then calculates a gross profit. Instead, the total direct product revenues and costs of each value stream are shown (e.g., materials, labor (which includes all labor), supplies, depreciation, and shipping). Then a value stream profit is determined before inventory is taken into consideration. Very few costs are allocated; most are direct costs of the value stream. The costs that serve all value streams are listed in a separate column for plant/company expenses. The unadjusted profit figure is then adjusted for changes in inventory. This high-lighting of the inventory effects is very important, since reducing inventory can have a negative effect on profitability figures—even though that is the behavior that lean firms are seeking. It also shows that some increases in profitability may actually be obtained by increasing inventory, which should be a negative assessment. Any corporate allocations and administrative expenses are separated from the value stream income and expense analysis. For an example of a plain English P&L, refer to Chapter 4.

Step 4: Decide on Changeover Date

A critical question in deciding to make an internal accounting change is when to transition your accounting system. How far along in your lean implementation should you be? How fully do you make the transition? Should you run parallel systems when you initially change your reporting system? All of these questions need to be addressed, and there isn't a simple or pat answer to any of them. Most companies are quite far into developing a lean culture throughout their organization before they consider changing their internal accounting reporting system. We don't necessarily think that is a good thing—it is just the more common practice. Of course, it is difficult to change to value stream costing without being first organized into value streams. Further, the accountants are less likely to support changing their traditional management accounting system if they have not participated in some of the lean initiatives and don't understand and feel a part of the lean culture. But if the groundwork has been laid in the company and in the accounting department, then the sooner you implement lean accounting, the better you are going to understand and appreciate the results from your lean improvements. In addition, you want to eliminate all that waste of tracking individual product costs and preparing unused and incomprehensible accounting reports as soon as possible.

A logical transition date is at your fiscal year-end. This way you have a beginning inventory figure that you trust, because it is how you have always calculated it. You can develop a method for valuing inventory through a simple, lean accounting process and make sure the ending inventory figure matches with your traditional inventory figure to start the new year. Your P&L is blank, so you can move to value stream costing and the new plain English format for the new year. For the first few months or even the first year, you may have to maintain your records under both the traditional and the lean system. Even though this may seem wasteful and anti lean, it provides assurance to your associates, corporate, and your auditors that the numbers you are producing under the lean system are materially in line with the numbers you would have produced under the traditional system. The advantages of the new lean system are mainly the elimination of wasteful transactions, inaccurate allocations to individual product lines, redundant financial reports, and formats that nonaccountants do not understand. But your total inventories should be materially the same using both the traditional and the lean accounting methods. Not every organization needs to initially run (wasteful) parallel systems. If you and your auditors are confident in your new inventory valuation approach, your inventories are relatively stable, and your turns are upwards of 12, then the risks of misstating inventory under the new system are minimal.

Step 5: Other Issues to Consider

It is very difficult for most accountants who have been steeped in traditional cost accounting to believe that you can basically do away with tracking individual product line margins and still have control of your operations and have adequate information for decision making. The traditional standard costing system with allocated overhead costs to each individual product via labor hours has been used for decades to get an "accurate" picture of what a product costs. Even though it is assumed that this is the easiest method for determining product costs, it is actually very costly, since organizations must track each labor hour that is worked and tie it to individual products. However, there are some instances when special processes or times spent at constraints (monuments) need to be evaluated for specific products. This is sometimes referred to as features and characteristics costing in lean accounting vernacular, and is explained in more detail in Chapter 7. For decision-making purposes, those products using more of your critical constraints should be assigned higher costs.

Oftentimes companies need to determine whether or not they can take on additional orders or whether they should outsource or in-source a product. These decisions are generally tied to resource capacity. In traditional accounting environments, companies will generally compare the additional revenues to the standard costs of a product and make their decision according to the new expected product margin. If the product margin of the new order or in-sourced product is reduced, then it will not be accepted. However, the real issue is whether or not you have excess capacity to build the product. The traditional method treats the standard cost as a variable cost, but the majority of product costs are really fixed—that includes most labor over a certain range. Thus, the analysis should be focused only on capacity and incremental costs incurred due to the additional business. (See Chapter 7 for an example of this decision-making process.)

Some facilities are pioneers in lean accounting in their organizations. The company may be transitioning to lean accounting plant by plant. Or there may be a "maverick" in the company that recognizes the need to simplify its accounting system and obtain more appropriate information. If either of these situations exists, then corporate may be accounting under the traditional method and individual plants using lean accounting. Under these circumstances, there must be a reconciliation of plant accounting to corporate accounting. It is critical to keep corporate abreast of your methods and hopefully obtain their commitment to the accounting changes. Oftentimes, corporate doesn't really care how you handle your internal accounting; they just want information that will fit in with the company information, and of course they don't want you to do anything that might hurt the proverbial bottom line.

The main issues to be addressed are inventory valuation and variance reporting. We have discussed inventory valuation issues earlier. Even though the approach to value inventory is easier than under the traditional method, it should result in materially the same amount as the traditional method. Thus, the reconciliation should be relatively straightforward, with a journal entry involving amounts to or from inventory. If you eliminate your standard costing system, you will not be reporting variances for conversion costs, and corporate will have to accept that. We are aware of one company whose plant manager was a lone champion for lean accounting. Corporate appeared to tolerate his methods. In the corporate financial reports that showed results for the individual plants, the line item for "budgeted absorption variance" was blank for his operations. The good news is that his persistence at demonstrating how well a simplified accounting system works in a lean environment is slowly capturing the attention of other divisions within the company.

There may be other issues that you face as an organization that we have not addressed. Since lean accounting is an emerging methodology, it is not likely that even the majority of issues and circumstances have been foreseen. But that also allows the flexibility and creativity of pioneering organizations to determine how the simplification and relevance of accounting information can be adapted to best fit their company.

Step 6: Review the Process

The mantra of lean is continuous improvement. Lean accounting is no different. Thus, you should always be looking for ways to improve your accounting processes and methods. You may find that what you initially thought would work well is either too simple or too complex for making quality decisions. If circumstances change in your business, you may have to have different information than what you originally planned. It is important to continually check with your customers to make sure they have the right information when they need it— and are no longer supplied with information overload or results that have little meaning or application to them. Kaizen events are excellent tools for improving accounting processes and reporting methods. Use them with cross-functional teams to stay aware of informational needs and improvement options.

Potential Obstacles in Transitioning Your Management Accounting System

Most people like stability and resist change. They are afraid of the unknown, and they can deal with what they are accustomed to, even if they know it may not be their best alternative. Making a dramatic change to an internal accounting system that has deep traditional roots is a major challenge. To jump on board, people have to understand the need for change and be assured that their jobs will remain intact and that the organization will not experience chaos. This requires education and marketing of the new system, as well as an explanation for why the old system is outdated and inappropriate. It is best if top management can facilitate the change with enthusiasm and optimism. If top management is antagonistic, success is unlikely; if top management is indifferent, then it takes a lean champion to lead the way. Of course, the accountants must be the change agents, and yet they may be the most resistant. It is our experience that accountants are generally risk averse and often comfortable crunching their numbers the way they have in the past. Since they were trained in traditional methods and most of their peers use traditional standard costing, they may be some of the most skeptical change participants.

The most common statement heard from those who challenge the need for change is, "Well, you don't understand. Our company is different." We are certain that your company is "different"; it is probably as unique as every other company. While some organizations may be more complex and others more conducive to a leaner reporting system, with some creativity and effort, simplifications and improvements can be made to all systems. It may take external eyes to help determine how to solve some of the change issues, but it is almost certain that a simpler, more effective internal reporting system can be designed to better support your lean operations.

A valid concern is the lack of understanding or training on how to make an accounting transition. You certainly don't want to lose all of your controls or your benchmarks or put your organization into any kind of external reporting jeopardy. Thus, you want to proceed with the proper training, evaluation, and experimentation. You may need to invest initially in external consultants to aid you with your transition. You can benchmark with others who have adopted lean accounting and locate available reading material to better educate those involved in the transition.

In order to get support for the transition, you must build confidence in the new system. You must prepare your organization for the changes that will occur in the financial reports. There will be fewer reports, and they will be simpler, but some may feel that implies they are less helpful. Also, reduced inventories that generally result from lean initiatives can often have an initial negative impact on margins and profitability. This potential effect must be carefully explained ahead of the event, so that management and shareholders are not surprised. But be sure to also remind them that cash flows should increase as you reduce the purchase of unnecessary buffer inventories. Further, some trend analysis and benchmarks may be lost as variances are eliminated and individual product margins are no longer calculated. Again, education about the expectations and the reasons for the new system is critical. To build confidence, some companies may need to run parallel systems with the old and the new for a few transitional months, as explained earlier.

Ideally, corporate is well informed of the needs for a new internal reporting system and, in fact, highly supportive of it. But if that is not the case, you may feel some push-back from corporate if they do not understand what you are trying to do. They, too, must be educated and forewarned about any financial effects that may occur. As long as business is going well, there is a fairly seamless transition, and the auditors have cleared the new system, you will probably not find much resistance. But even if there is not much resistance from corporate, if a plant is taking this charge on its own, it will take strong commitment from the leaders of that plant to make the transition successful. We have watched some plant managers experience "bullying" tactics from corporate and other naysayers in trying to block change. However, as the benefits are realized and companies become more motivated and efficient in their lean efforts, we have witnessed those naysayers become proponents—and even marketers of lean accounting methods to other divisions.

As mentioned several times in this discussion, it is critical to inform your external auditors about any financial reporting changes. To our knowledge, lean accounting has not been a hurdle for any audits. In fact, inventory valuations under lean accounting, which would be the primary concern for auditors, should be more accurate than traditional standard costing because they are calculated with direct, actual costs and not allocations.

Benefits of a Lean Accounting System

If there weren't substantial expected benefits from transitioning your accounting system, there would be little reason to consider such a move. Once operational, lean accounting should free up resources to be used elsewhere. The money and time used to track work orders with labor hours and overhead rates throughout the operations will no longer be necessary. Thus, IT systems can be simplified and labor hours formerly used for tracking transactions will be reduced. Accountants should have more time to use their considerable talents in more auspicious ways—aid in strategic planning, participate in all types of process improvements, and help in developing an appropriate visual performance measurement system. There will be fewer reports to prepare, again saving computer time, labor time, and supply costs.

Lean accounting motivates more appropriate behaviors for lean environments, whereas traditional variances encourage workers to work as fast as they can and to fully utilize machine resources. The more you produce, the better the variances look; there is no consideration for demand—only production. Remember, this is a mindset that inventories are assets, so the more product we build, the stronger our balance sheet becomes. Even our P&L looks better as we build more product, because we can move some of those fixed product costs onto the balance sheet. While lean accounting does not solve all of these misguided motivations, it does resolve some of them by eliminating variance analysis. It also helps management better understand the effects of full absorption costing required by GAAP for inventory valuation through highlighting the inventory change effects on the plain English P&L. Further, lean accounting focuses on direct costs rather than allocated standard costs in trying to make value streams efficient and cost-effective. Decision making is improved and more straightforward by examining only the incremental effects on the value stream of expanded product lines, in-sourcing, additional orders, and capacity constraints.

Lean accounting is more customer focused. Rather than burdening management with information overload and financial reports in "accounting speak," the reports are minimized to those that are really needed and used, with terms and formats that are simple and easy for everyone to understand. Management no longer has to decipher what created a volume variance, how to solve an unfavorable overhead variance, or what specifically made the gross profit margin decrease when sales increased. The information is clear and straightforward, as specific accounts are shown and trends can be easily interpreted. Value stream managers responsible for all of the costs that affect their value streams have a better understanding of what those costs are. They are not penalized for producing only to demand and eliminating obsolescent inventories, even though that may initially decrease their profitability. Management and accountants can communicate better, because managers are not expected to be proficient in some of the innuendoes found in the proverbial language of business.

Almost everyone in a typical organization understands that you don't bother the accountants at the end of the month. They are too busy closing their books. Of course, at year-end, their stress is escalated and overtime is rampant for a few weeks until the books are closed for the year. As many companies moving lean into their accounting systems have reported, it doesn't need to be like that. Examples abound of organizations improving their closing process times by several multiples of 100% using the concepts of lean thinking. Eliminating non-value-added work such as errors and unnecessary transactions will bring some immediate time reductions. Some of that will occur naturally as you transition to a lean accounting system. Many of the batch processes that are done at the end of the month can be changed to a flow mentality and performed automatically or during the month when more time is available (e.g., accounting for depreciation and reserves). Remember to be patient. You may have an ultimate goal of a one-day close, but reducing your closing time must happen in incremental process improvements over time.

Caution is given to all those that expect immediate dramatic results from lean and lean accounting. As suggested above, change has to occur incrementally and reasonably for your personnel to adapt and your organization to build the right culture. The benefits from change are sometimes subtle and slower to emerge than many would prefer. Lean, as with all transformational change, absolutely requires the 3 Ps: patience, pain, and perseverance.

Summary

We wouldn't be writing this book if we didn't strongly believe that the internal reporting systems of lean organizations need to be changed. Hopefully, we have provided you with some motivational and rational reasons for the need for change, as well as some guidelines into how to make the transition. However, currently, only a limited number of firms have embraced these concepts. Using primarily direct costs of a value stream and then calculating an average product cost per value stream is a radically new approach to product costing, so it is easy to see why companies are hesitant to "take the plunge." One of the authors took her graduate accounting class on a tour of a world-class lean facility that charges other companies for similar tours. At the end of the very impressive tour, they sat down in the conference room with the controller and heard about the company's internal accounting system. The company no longer assigns labor costs to individual products, or allocates overheads, or calculates conversion cost variances. The changes made to their accounting system were in response to their international parent company, which said it couldn't make sense of all the variance reporting. The parent company asked for simpler, more comprehensible financial reports—and that is what the controller designed. The controller also told us that visitors on the plant tours are enthusiastic about what they observe on the shop floor. But when the new, simpler, nontraditional internal accounting system is presented, people are apprehensive.

Why this reluctance to move to a simpler, more relevant internal reporting system? It is our belief that there are limited venues available to educate and train lean organizations about the potential and mechanisms of lean accounting. Further, it takes an entrepreneurial spirit for an organization to pursue leading-edge methods—whether those methods are on the shop floor or in the support departments. Lean manufacturing has been prevalent for around three decades now and has proven its worth. However, lean accounting is a relative newcomer on the block, even though cries for more relevant management accounting systems were published over 30 years ago.

Hopefully, after reading this material, you will have a clearer sense of what constitutes lean accounting, how it could serve your lean organization, and why we are so dedicated in teaching others about its potential. You may still be asking: If lean accounting is so effective and critical to a lean organization, why haven't more firms more fully and rapidly embraced its concepts. We don't have an adequate answer to that question, although we have tried to discuss some of the offsetting roadblocks to its presumed benefits. We are hoping that you may have that pioneering spirit to look for ways to improve your accounting information system, and that this workbook can help you start that process. As you progress through your lean journey, don't forget to take your accounting operations with you! We believe if you do so, you will be much more successful on that journey.

Discussion Questions

1. What characteristics should be in place before transitioning to a lean accounting system? Is this typically the same for every lean organization?
2. Why is it important for top management's support in a lean accounting transition? What can you do to encourage that support?
3. What concerns are there in making sure that your accounting transition is GAAP compliant?
4. What are some of the challenges of organizing by value streams?
5. How are product costs reported in a lean accounting system?
6. Discuss various methods and pitfalls of inventory valuation for a lean organization.

7. What are some of the differences between the internal reporting of a traditional accounting system and that of a lean accounting system?

8. Discuss some of the issues related to the transition period of an internal accounting system.

9. Why would a traditional internal accounting system be more costly and inaccurate than a lean accounting system?

10. Identify some of the critical issues to making a lean accounting system effective. What are some of the obstacles that you may face in the transition period?

11. Identify some of the costs and benefits of transitioning to a lean accounting system.

Appendix A: Glossary of Lean and Lean Accounting Terminology

5S: A five-step improvement process: sort (separate needed items from unneeded items), straighten (arrange needed items in a way that they are easy to find and near where used), shine (clean items and area), standardize (develop procedure for sorting, straightening, and shining), and sustain (continue to following 5S and encourage employees to do so too).

A3 (report): An A3 is a large piece of paper (normally 11 × 17). An A3 report is when a problem, analysis, possible actions, and an action plan are reported on a single A3. It is a summary of the project and normally includes graphics. The purpose is to quickly communicate project status.

Bottleneck: The point in the production line that allows the lowest amount of product through in a set time (throughput). It can become a problem if demand is greater than the amount that can be produced by the bottleneck.

Box score: A visual display of key actual and target metrics usually updated weekly. The box score typically includes operational, capacity, and financial measures.

Catchball: A process in which levels of an organization ensure that goals and strategies are understood and are feasible. First the higher level creates the goals and strategies and communicates them to the lower level, then the lower level interprets them and communicates them back to the higher level to ensure that everyone is on the same page. Often the lower level makes suggestions for change based on its more detailed knowledge.

Cellular manufacturing: Manufacturing in a cell, which is an area in which the machines needed for production are laid out in a logical and efficient way (normally sequentially in the production process) that allows for one-piece flow or small batches through multiple processes.

DMAIC: An improving process that is data driven; define, measure, analyze, improve, and control are the interconnected phases.

Features and characteristics costs: A costing method used only for transfer pricing and to estimate product pricing. In this method, unique costs, such as material, are added to conversion costs per unit to estimate a unit cost.

Gemba: A Japanese term for "the real place." It is used to describe going to the place that work is performed (i.e., the machine cell, the tool shop) to better understand the process.

Hoshin kanri: Policy management; upper management uses a strategic decision-making process to align the firm's activities and resources with its strategic objectives. Normally a plan is created annually and contains goals, action plans, timelines, responsibilities, and benchmarks.

Inventory turns: Annual cost of goods sold divided by average value of inventories during the year; a ratio that measure how quickly materials are being used.

Kaizen: "To take apart," "to make good." A process of continual improvement of a value stream or process, the goal of which is to add value while reducing waste.

Kanban: "Signboard," "signal." A visual signaling device that represents a certain quantity of material or parts and gives authorization and instructions in a pull system.

Monuments: Any machine or tool that cannot easily be moved and has long changeover times, and therefore designs, orders, or products must be brought to it and wait in a queue for processing.

Muda: A Japanese term for waste that is commonly used within companies.

Nemawashi: "Preparing the ground for planting." Getting preapproval for a proposal by evaluating the idea and plan with management and stakeholders and getting feedback and discussing possible resistance and how to align the proposal with other priorities of the organization.

PDCA: An improvement cycle with four stages: plan (plan change), do (implement change), check (evaluate results), and act (adjust plan, standardize change, or start over).

Poka-yoke: "Innocent mistake-proofing." A device or procedure to help workers not make mistakes in order taking or manufacturing.

Sensei: In a lean environment, a *sensei* is a highly knowledgeable and experienced authority in lean processes who is invited into a company to observe and suggest change. In general terms, sensei is likened to "master" or "teacher."

Standardized work: A precise set of procedures for each job in a production process, including the takt time, the work sequence, and the standard materials needed.

Takt time: Available production time divided by customer demand; the pace of production that needs to be achieved to meet customer demand.

Total productive maintenance (TPM): A set of techniques used company-wide to make sure that every machine in a production process is able to perform its tasks by getting employees involved in planning the design, selection, correction, and maintenance of the equipment.

Value stream maps: A basic diagram of the specific activities in the material and information flows from an order to the delivery of a product.

Visual management: A tool that allows everyone to understand the status of the system at a glance by placing in clear view all tools, parts, activities, and indicators of system performance.

X-Matrix: Used in policy deployment, *X-Matrix* is a method of visually linking each employee's goals with top level strategy.

Yamazumi boards: "Pile," "stack." A chart that can help find opportunities to improve total cycle time by visually displaying work elements, times, and assignments in a value stream.

Reference

Lean Enterprise Institute. 2006. *Lean lexicon: A graphical glossary for lean thinkers.* Lean Enterprise Institute, Cambridge, MA.

Appendix B: Lean Measurement Assessment Instrument

Performance Measure Assessment for the Lean Enterprise

Background

The ideal scenario for a company who is transitioning from traditional production methods to lean practices is to completely reconstruct the performance measurement system to reflect the new value stream organization. Strategically aligning performance measures through a well-defined process is an important key to a successful transition. Unfortunately, completely revamping the measurement system is not always feasible right out of the gate. There may be resistance to radical changes, particularly when some measures may be tied to incentive systems. There is, however, still a need to assess current measures to determine which ones promote lean thinking and which ones do not.

Purpose

The purpose of this instrument is to logically assess measures currently used in your organization considering the five principles of lean thinking: value, value stream, flow and pull, empowerment, and perfection.[*]

In addition to the principles of lean thinking, this instrument methodically assesses the effectiveness of each metric based on the attributes of a good measure: technical, behavioral, and cultural.[†] Attributes are the inherent characteristics embedded within a measure that influences the interpretation and potential actions of the user.

There are two primary benefits to this instrument. The first is that it provides a scaled assessment of how well individual metrics serve your organization. The second is that it promotes logical and thoughtful discussion of the measures'

---

[*] These principles are adapted from James P. Womack and Daniel T. Jones in their book *Lean Thinking: Banish Waste and Create Wealth in Your Corporation* (New York: Simon and Schuster, 1996).

[†] The attributes of a good measure are outlined in *Strategy and Management Accounting*, by Shahid Asari, Jan Bell, Thomas Klammer, and Carol Lawrence (Boston: Houghton Mifflin, 1996).

characteristics. This additional analysis offers insight into strengths or limitations of current measures.

Directions

The instrument* contains three sections—one for each attribute: technical, behavioral, and cultural. Each section contains a brief summary of the attribute and a list of questions. These questions are designed to encourage you to thoughtfully consider individual characteristics of the measure. At the bottom of each section are four questions that ask you to reflect upon your answers and score the effectiveness of the measure with regard to that attribute. Once you have completed all three sections, you will have an average score for each of the attributes of the measure. The following graph is an example of the information it may provide:

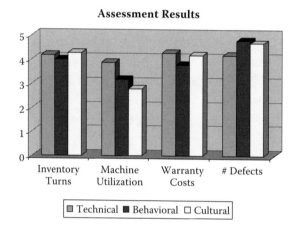

---

* The instrument was developed and published by F. Kennedy, L. Owens-Jackson, and M. Schoon in "How Do Your Measurements Stack Up to Lean?" *Strategic Finance*, May 2007, pp. 32–41.

METRIC ASSESSMENT

Measure _____How frequently is the measure provided?

Calculation _____

> **SECTION 1: Technical Attributes** refer to the measurement-related qualities desired in the information. There are two key properties of good measures: *Decision Relevance* and *Process Understanding*. Information is relevant to a decision *IF* the information changes *AND* improves the quality of decisions. Measures increase process understanding if they consider an entire process rather than a single functional unit. This is because work flows horizontally across units and functional measures do not provide information needed to perform work.

	QUESTION	ANSWER
T1	Who uses this measurement information?	
T2	What decisions does the measurement inform?	
T3	Does the metric change between periods (e.g., quarterly or annually)?	
T4	Is it a functional or process-oriented measure (e.g., single department or multiple departments)?	
T5	Does this measure promote a smooth work flow?	
T6	Is the measure related to a bottleneck* process?	
T7	Does this measure relate to product or service quality?	
T8	Does the measure provide information on the causes of defects?	
T9	Does this measure relate to customer service?	
T10	What activity driver† does this metric measure?	
T11	Which costs does this measure monitor?	
T12	How major or minor is this cost with respect to total production costs?	

Review your answers to the questions relating to the technical characteristics of this measure (T1–T12). Evaluate using the following criteria. Score your answers according to the extent to which you agree with the statement.

This measure . . .

		Strongly Disagree				Strongly Agree
1	provides information that helps to manage cost, quality, and/or customer service.	1	2	3	4	5
2	adds to the user's knowledge base.	1	2	3	4	5
3	adds to th user's understanding of the process.	1	2	3	4	5
4	provides information concerning the sources of problems.	1	2	3	4	5
5	provides information that is relevant to the decision in question.	1	2	3	4	5

AVERAGE SCORE_____

---

*A bottleneck is a stage in the production that delays the movement of material through the process.
†An activity driver is any measurable factor that causes a change in the cost of an activity.

SECTION 2: **Behavioral Attributes** refer to the ways that measurements affect behavior by making information visible. Measurement communicates importance and signals priorities. As a result, employees are motivated to manage their behavior and output in order to improve those measures.

	QUESTION	ANSWER
B1	How does this measure relate to employee work or output (e.g., quality, throughput)?	
B2	How does this measure relate to the firm's strategic goals?	
B3	Where does the measure focus attention?	
B4	What behavior is the measure attempting to motivate (e.g., smooth flow)?	
B5	What behavior does the measure actually motivate?	
B6	What group behavior does the measure motivate (e.g., produce volume, investigate quality problems, instill ownership and pride)?	
B7	What individual employee behavior does the measure motivate (e.g., signal for help, ridicule, or envy)?	
B8	Do the users of this measure understand its calculation, definition, and purpose?	
B9	How well is the measurement goal communicated?	
B10	What is the reward for goal achievement?	
B11	Who is held accountable for this measure?	
B12	Do those employees held accountable for the measure have control over the factors affecting the measure?	

Review your answers to the questions relating to the behavioral characteristics of this measure (B1–B12). Evaluate using the following criteria. Score your answers according to the extent to which you agree with the statement.

This measure . . .

		Strongly Disagree				Strongly Agree
1	provides information on how well one or more strategic goals are achieved.	1	2	3	4	5
2	motivates desired behavior.	1	2	3	4	5
3	evaluates the performance of only those employees able to effect change in the metric.	1	2	3	4	5
4	conveys clearly to the users how the measure is calculated.	1	2	3	4	5
5	conveys clearly to the users target expectations.	1	2	3	45	

AVERAGE SCORE _____

SECTION 3: Cultural Attributes refer to the beliefs, values, and mindsets embedded in a measure. Measures are symbols that represent mindsets held by members of organizations and unconsciously guide sustainable behavior without the need for punishment or rewards. Employees use their belief system to interpret the meaning of accounting measures and determine what actions should be taken. For example, an organization steeped in lean practices would not successfully be able to introduce a measure that encouraged building excess inventory. The following questions consider the characteristics ingrained in a lean enterprise.

	QUESTION	ANSWER
C1	How does this measure reflect the belief system of the company (e.g., fiscal prudence, lean practices, high quality)?	
C2	Does the measure encourage behavior that conflicts with ethical behavior?	
C3	How does this measure reflect value as defined from the customer's viewpoint?	
C4	Does this measure promote thinking about the entire value stream* or does it focus on an individual department/cell†?	
C5	Does this measure encourage one piece flow through the production cell?	
C6	Does this measure encourage minimizing inventory or building inventory?	
C7	Does this measure provide adequate information to the people making the decision (e.g., cell or value stream)?	
C8	Does this measure promote continuous improvement at the cell and/or value stream level?	
C9	Does this measure promote the elimination of unnecessary steps and/or waste?	

Review your answers to the questions relating to the cultural characteristics of this measure (C1–C9). Evaluate using the following criteria. Score your answers according to the extent to which you agree with the statement.

This measure . . .

		Strongly Disagree				Strongly Agree
1	provides information on process factors affecting customer value.	1	2	3	4	5
2	provides information that promotes thinking about the process or value stream as a whole.	1	2	3	4	5
3	promotes continuous improvement.	1	2	3	4	5
4	identifies and/or eliminates waste.	1	2	3	4	5
5	ensures that employees who make decisions have adequate information.	1	2	3	4	5

AVERAGE SCORE _____

*A value stream represents all the things a business does to create value for the customer. A typical business-wide value stream includes all activities from the sales order entry to after sales support.
†A cell is a structural or functional unit within a production process.

Index

About the Authors

Gloria McVay is a professor of accounting at Winona State University, where she teaches managerial and strategic cost accounting courses, including a course on accounting for the lean enterprise. She was the first professor to receive the Excellence in Lean Accounting Professor Award from the Lean Enterprise Institute. Dr. McVay's primary areas of research and practice include lean accounting, lean in healthcare, and improvements in instructional design for all types of learners. Her academic perspective is sharpened by her work with actual companies on their lean journeys. She has presented her research at numerous international conferences in the United States, Mexico, and Europe.

Dr. McVay has a PhD in accounting from the University of Kentucky and a BS and MBA from Minnesota State University, Mankato. Prior to her academic career, she managed a billion-dollar pension fund at Ceridian Corporation and held various accounting and finance positions with Henkel of America, including pension fund management, cash management, and senior financial analysis. Dr. McVay began her professional career as an auditor with Arthur Andersen.

Frances Kennedy is the director of the School of Accountancy and Finance at Clemson University, where she also teaches managerial accounting. She gained her manufacturing experience as an accounting manager in a manufacturing plant, as a division financial liaison with multiple plants, and as a financial analyst on a new product development team. Dr. Kennedy's research focuses on performance measurements and control systems in lean enterprises, and she has been published in both academic and professional journals. She has presented her research in lean and performance measurements at professional and academic conferences in several countries.

Dr. Kennedy earned her PhD in accounting from the University of North Texas in 2001 and has been at Clemson ever since. Thirteen years of experience in public accounting as a CPA and in industry enriches her teaching and informs her research. Dr. Kennedy was presented the 2009 Lean Six Sigma Leadership Award from the International Lean Six Sigma Conference and the Lean Accounting Summit's 2007 award recognizing her efforts to promote lean accounting in both the classroom and the profession. Dr. Kennedy is also the 2006 recipient of the Silver Lybrand Medal, awarded by the Institute of Management Accountants, and the 2006 Award of Merit, from the International Federation of Accountants, for her contributions to the field of management accounting.

Rosemary Fullerton is the Arthur Andersen Alumni Professor of Accounting in the Jon M. Huntsman School of Business at Utah State University (USU), where she teaches undergraduate strategic cost management and graduate advanced management accounting, focusing on lean principles and lean accounting. Dr. Fullerton's research interests include investigating the prevalence of lean accounting and its impact on lean manufacturing environments. She has presented her research at numerous universities and conferences throughout the United States and in Canada and Europe. She has also presented multiple seminars on lean accounting to both professional and academic audiences around the country.

Dr. Fullerton is affiliated with the Shingo Prize for Operational Excellence, serving as a member of the Shingo Prize Board of Examiners. In 2011, she was the recipient of the Utah Association of CPAs Outstanding Educator Award and the Excellence in Lean Accounting Professor Award from the Lean Enterprise Institute. She has won two Shingo Research Prizes, including one for her book, *Accounting for World Class Operations* (coauthored with Jerry Solomon). Dr. Fullerton obtained a PhD from the University of Utah, a BS and MAcc from Utah State University, a BA in English from Brigham Young University, and is a licensed CPA in the state of Utah. In addition to USU, she taught for one year at McGill University in Montreal, Canada. Prior to her academic career, Dr. Fullerton worked as a CPA for Davis & Bott, CPAs, in Brigham City, Utah.